Re:Mission

Re:Mission

Biblical Mission for a Post-Biblical Church

Andrew Perriman

Paternoster:
thinking faith

MILTON KEYNES ● COLORADO SPRINGS ● HYDERABAD

First published 2007 by Authentic Media
9 Holdom Avenue, Bletchley, Milton Keynes, Bucks, MK1 1QR, UK
1820 Jet Stream Drive, Colorado Springs, CO 80921, USA
OM Authentic Media, Medchal Road, Jeedimetla Village,
Secunderabad 500 055, A.P., India
www.authenticmedia.co.uk

Authentic Media is a division of IBS-STL U.K., limited by guarantee, with its
Registered Office at Kingstown Broadway, Carlisle, Cumbria CA3 0HA.
Registered in England & Wales No. 1216232. Registered charity 270162

British Library Cataloguing in Publication Data

A catalogue record for this book is available from the British Library

ISBN-13: 978-1-84227-545-0

Design by James Kessel for Scratch the Sky Ltd (www.scratchthesky.com)
Print Management by Adare Carwin
Printed and bound in Great Britain by J.H. Haynes & Co., Sparkford

For Samuel,
in appreciation of journeys around a small world

Contents

Faith in an Emerging Culture
Series Preface

It is common knowledge that Western culture has undergone major changes and we now find ourselves in an increasingly postmodern (or post-postmodern?), post-Christendom, post-industrial, post-just-about-anything-you-like world. The church now sits on the margins of Western culture with a faith 'package deal' to offer the world that is perceived as out of date and irrelevant. How can we recontextualize the old, old story of the gospel in the new, new world of postmodernity? How can we fulfill our missional calling in a world that cannot any longer understand or relate to what we are saying? 'Faith in an Emerging Culture' seeks to imaginatively rethink Christian theology and practice in postmodern ways. It does not shrink from being explorative, provocative, and controversial but is at the same time committed to remaining within the bounds of orthodox Christian faith and practice. Most readers will find things to agree with and things which will irritate them but we hope at the very least to provoke fresh thought and theological/spiritual renewal.

1

Re: Re:Mission

Let me begin by describing three 'missional' projects that I know a bit about. I mention them as instances of a trend, not because there is anything exceptional about them. First, a community of faith called Mosaic in Glasgow, Scotland, currently spends one Sunday morning a month helping to clean up the Kelvin River, which flows twenty-two miles from Dullatur Bog to the Clyde. They do this under the supervision of a local charity, Friends of the River Kelvin. They regard the activity as both worship and mission: 'We believe that words alone are not sufficient; how the gospel is embodied in our community and service is as important as what we say. Whether it be cleaning up the Kelvin River, sharing our struggles, or helping someone in the community move house, we are participating in the Mission of God.'[1]

Secondly, The Well in Brussels describes itself as 'church, but not a building or a meeting.'[2] Their emphasis on drinking from the life of Jesus and journeying through life together as community is characteristic of the emerging church movement. So too is their stated mission and the small 'g' for God: 'to serve people in need and care for god's world that his kingdom may come on earth as it is in heaven.' This 'church, but not a building or a meeting' defines its missional orientation principally through an annual project called Serve the City, which brings together volunteers from other churches in Brussels and from around the world to run a variety of neighborhood activities, from a basketball camp for kids to 'massaging Congolese mammas.'

Thirdly, I have been involved with a few people from Crossroads International Church in The Hague, the Netherlands, in running what we call a 'Soul Party.'[3] It is a monthly event where people of faith and no faith can get together and talk about things that matter. 'It's a party . . . with a certain ambience or mood, with a theme running through it, a controversy, a challenge, something to think about, talk about, get excited about . . . something that touches the soul. Life. Pain. Joy. Beauty. Mystery. Love.' It is not an outreach event; it takes place on strictly neutral ground. The most it is, on our part, is a gift of friendship and conversation – but inasmuch as it's *our* gift, I would call it 'missional.'

The practical question behind this book is, How do we connect activities such as these, and perhaps more importantly the instincts and assumptions that motivate them, with the biblical narrative? Can they genuinely be called 'missional'? Do they have a legitimate foundation in Scripture, or are they just further examples of rudderless groups of believers being blown out of the mainstream of biblical mission by the winds of culture? Dragging rusty supermarket trolleys out of the River Kelvin will strike many Christians as a questionable form of worship and a highly ineffective way of saving souls. Serve the City may be an honest, energetic attempt to love one's neighborhood, but does it really have anything to do with the kingdom of God? What good does it do for The Well to pour a few buckets of water onto a desert of social need from time to time? A 'Soul Party' sounds funky and a great way for Christians to get out a bit more, but can 'strictly neutral ground' really be 'missional'?

There is a big theological conundrum lurking in the shadows here. What does the church have to do with the created order? Do such concerns and interests as environmental care and social justice, the deep and disturbing powers of imagination and creativity, the culture and wisdom of humanity, really come within the purview of its calling?

A rather different question is raised by the phrase 'post-biblical church' in the subtitle of this book. Post-biblical? The issue here is this: How does the church relate to the narrative of the New Testament and in particular to the narrative *as it is projected into the future*? We normally assume that the teaching of the New Testament can be applied directly, even if sometimes selectively, to the circumstances of the church today. So when Jesus or Paul says, 'This is what you are, or what you should think, or how you should behave,' we take that to be as true and relevant for us today as for the early communities of Christ-followers. A theology, however, which gives priority not to the formal, ordered content of belief but to *narrative* structures and in particular to the close interaction between narrative and history, is bound to question that assumption. It raises the serious possibility that the church today is *not* in the same situation as the church in the first century, that we are at a rather different place in the story line – indeed, that we have traveled across mountain ranges into territory that was largely out of sight to the authors of the New Testament. Real narratives do not stop, even when we reach the fairy-tale wedding. So we would have to address the question of identity and purpose not by reading the New Testament as a blueprint for the church at all times and in all places but by following the narrative trajectory of what is usually known as 'eschatology' – the early community's expectation of decisive transformation at some future point.[4] In this way it should be possible to construct a genuinely *biblical* theology of mission for a post-biblical church.

In *The Coming of the Son of Man* I argued that when the New Testament looks into the future, it sees, in effect, three horizons.[5] The first is marked by the disastrous war against Rome and the destruction of Jerusalem in AD 70. Most of Jesus' teaching, including his difficult but crucial apocalyptic discourse, has this horizon in view. The second is less sharply defined, partly because it relates to a more complex geopolitical situation, partly because it belongs to a more distant future. It consists, on the one hand, of the collapse of Roman imperialism as an idolatrous and unjust ideology radically opposed to the people of YHWH and, on the other, of the elevation of Christ to a place of cosmic authority *above Caesar* – that is certainly part of what

Paul means when he says that Jesus has been given the name which is above every name (Phil. 2:9). At a historical level it is this concrete political-religious realignment that is signified by the *parousia* motif in Paul. For the most part New Testament eschatology is preoccupied with these first two horizons. The third horizon of a final judgement of all the dead and renewal of creation is barely discerned beyond the dark billowing visions of impending crisis. We will consider the implications of this schematization later, but for now a simple diagram may be helpful.

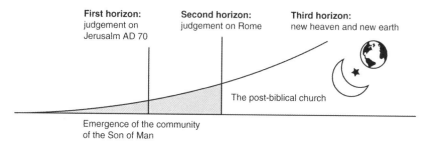

First horizon: Second horizon: Third horizon:
judgement on   judgement on Rome   new heaven and new earth
Jerusalm AD 70

The post-biblical church

Emergence of the community
of the Son of Man

Figure 1.1 Horizons of New Testament eschatology

It is as we move beyond the biblical space, as the third horizon comes into view, that the narrative question and the theological question merge. As we trace the New Testament story across the uneven and sometimes quite precipitous landscape of history, as we listen to the immediate hopes and anxieties of the communities involved, as we gain a clearer sense of how this story is itself only a painful episode in a much older story, I think we will find that the question of mission will come to appear in a rather different light. I will suggest that *in the first place* words and phrases such as 'gospel,' 'salvation,' 'redemption,' 'evangelism,' and 'kingdom of God' – the common currency of mission – do not denote universal, personal categories; they refer to concrete and contingent moments in the historical narrative of the people of God. At least, we are likely to misuse them if we do not first understand how they work *narratively* and how the narrative sets contextual boundaries to their meaning. Similarly, the classic mission texts – the so-called 'Great Commission' of Matthew 28:18–20, for example – are story-bound, and we risk doing serious damage to them if we tear them from the narrative in our eagerness to construct a coherent and teachable doctrine of mission. Whether the terminology and texts can be used in a secondary, perhaps extended or analogical, sense is a matter for subsequent discussion. For the time being we need to wear blinkers.

So we put the historical existence of the people of God at center stage, which means we must begin with Abraham. We will have to ask why at this moment in the story of humanity the Creator God brings into existence a nation that will be fruitful and multiply in a fertile land, that will be blessed and be a blessing to all the families of the earth. We will need to understand what happens to this re-creational initiative and how eventually the descendants of Abraham end up under Roman rule, facing political disaster. At this point we will see how a different story starts to be told – the story of an emerging community *in Christ* that will suffer under the tumultuous conditions of the end of the age *for the sake of the re-creational initiative*, for the sake of the promise to Abraham. This community is called to walk a difficult road of faithfulness, first through the crisis of Israel's disintegration, then through the protracted and sporadic conflicts with Greek–Roman paganism, until its 'enemies' are overcome and it stands vindicated before the throne of God. This is the climax of the story of the Son of Man, but it is only the recovery of the story of the re-creational initiative, the recovery of the promise to Abraham. We will have to be careful not to confuse these two narratives: an overarching story about the renewal of creation and an intercalated story about the salvation of the people who are called to be new creation in the midst of the nations and cultures of the earth.

When the creational story picks up again, following the victory of the saints of the Most High over the arch-opponent of YHWH, it takes on the historical character and dimensions of Christendom. Rightly or wrongly – and certainly ironically – the church that emerged from the conflict with Rome assumed over time the shape and ambitions of empire, both in political and in intellectual terms. This paradigm survived in various forms and iterations well into the twentieth century, but it is now in an advanced state of collapse. At risk of gross oversimplification, I would suggest that, whether we realize it or not, we are currently engaged in the development of a new paradigm by which the post-Christendom, post-modern people of God may embody the re-creational initiative which is at the heart of what we call – somewhat inappropriately – 'mission.' This cannot be done simply by attempting to imitate the New Testament church: we are in a proper sense *beyond that*. We must understand how the stories of creation and salvation interact in Scripture and how that interaction impels us into an unknown future.

New Testament thought is structured around an eschatological narrative core that gives, for the most part, forward-looking definition to a critical and painful transition in the history of the people of God. In our typical formulations of the identity and purpose of the church we have collapsed this lengthy narrative down to a two-dimensional existential gospel that seriously distorts both the scope and, I would argue, the credibility of the story that the church needs to tell about itself. We are left with a simplistic prescription for the 'life of the age to come' which isolates Jesus' death and resurrection not only from his prophetic engagement with Israel but also from the historical experience of the people of God, which makes personal salvation the more or less exclusive focus of mission, and which reduces hope to the remote prospect of life with God in heaven. The eschatological narrative needs to be recovered and put back in the larger story of the people of God in such a way that not only its intense transformative significance but also its boundaries are properly recognized and understood.

This is a book about mission (re: mission), but it is a rethinking of what mission means (re-mission) in the light of a realistic eschatology that flies close to the ground of history. This gives rise to the insight that the story of the forgiveness (remission) of Israel's sins sits inside a larger narrative about the calling of a people to be in the fullest sense an authentic humanity. These interlocking stories are told in this book, but not – I would warn – with the attention to exegetical detail and comprehensiveness of theological argumentation that serious-minded theologians might expect to find. The more detailed argument of *The Coming of the Son of Man* is presupposed at a number of points, but much of the support needed to defend the reading must be imagined to lie beneath the surface of the text. This is, in the first place, an exercise in storytelling – because the story is where all theology begins, because we have lost sight of the narrative structure of biblical thought, and because the church must see itself in the world not least as a storytelling community.

2

Two Bedtime Stories and a Preview of Paul's Argument in Romans

The trickster Jacob is on the run. He has fled from the anger of his brother Esau, having defrauded him of his birthright, and is traveling to Haran to stay with his uncle Laban. Until things cool down. And perhaps he will find a wife while he is there. Near the city of Luz, sleeping beneath the desert sky, his head resting heavily on a stone, he has a dream in which he sees what was probably not a ladder but a great ramp of earth, or a staircase, reaching up to heaven; and the 'angels of God were ascending and descending on it' (Gen. 28:12). We should picture something like a Mesopotamian ziggurat, a squat pyramid, with a broad flight of steps leading to its summit, not an overextended ladder bowing precariously between heaven and earth with the angels clinging on for dear life. In the dream God appears above the staircase and repeats for Jacob's benefit the promise that was originally made to Abraham: the land on which he lies will be given to him; his offspring will be like the dust of the earth and will spread throughout the land; and through them all the families of the earth will be blessed.

This curious, ancient image of a stairway from heaven reappears unexpectedly at the beginning of John's Gospel. Philip wants to introduce Nathanael to Jesus – the one of whom 'Moses in the Law and also the prophets wrote' (John 1:45). When Jesus tells the guileless Nathanael that he saw him and recognized him when he was still under the fig tree, Nathanael can hardly contain himself: 'Rabbi, you are the Son of God! You are the King of Israel!' But, Jesus tells him, he will see greater things than these. Indeed, he will see heaven opened, and the 'angels of God ascending and descending on the Son of Man' (John 1:51). The allusion to Jacob's dream is unmistakable, but what does it mean? How are we to make sense of Jesus' assertion that Nathanael and others (the verb is plural) will see something very much like what Jacob saw? And why, apparently, has Jacob been replaced by the 'Son of Man'?

These questions will take us to the heart of the argument of this book, but they also highlight a couple of issues related to *how* we read the New Testament that need to be considered first.

The first has to do with the allusiveness of the New Testament. How do we make sense of the countless fragments of the Jewish Scriptures that turn up, like shards of broken pottery, wherever we sift through its complex stratified discourse? How do they contribute to the meaning of the passage? I want to argue strongly that we need to do more with these broken pieces of Old Testament texts than simply catalogue them. We need almost always to understand the whole artifact from which they derive; we need to reconstruct the item of pottery in our minds as we read, we need to see its shape, determine the use to which it might have been put, and perhaps decipher the ancient story that is being told in the stylized frieze painted on its surface. So, for example, when Jesus makes use of the language of Jacob's dream we should assume that he does so quite purposefully and that he expects the larger story to be heard as part of the argument. Flick the small verbal switch in the New Testament, and a whole passage – an argument, an open-ended story – lights up in the Jewish Scriptures. To grasp what Jesus is saying to Nathanael and the others we must read the account of Jacob's journey into exile; we must ask about the significance of his dream for that story; and then we must ask how that significance is utilized within the narrative of the gospel. Similarly, if we are to make sense of the reference to the Son of Man we must explore the narrative of suffering and vindication that is encapsulated in Daniel's vision of a figure in human form coming on the clouds of heaven.

There are certainly problems with this approach. It is not always clear whether a word or phrase is really meant to invoke a particular Old Testament text. And if it does, we will still need to make a difficult judgement about how much of the original context is relevant for interpretation and in what way. But we should assume that Old Testament texts generally provide a relevant context of meaning for the words, phrases, quotations, and para-phrases that litter the pages of the New Testament. In the end the validity of the method will be determined to a large degree by the overall coherence and credibility of the reading that emerges.

Secondly, when Jesus says that Nathanael and the others will 'see' the angels of God ascending and descending on the Son of Man, I take it that he does not mean this literally. He means, roughly, that they will see or experience the *significance* of Jacob's dream fulfilled in their own future – and in relation to the Son of Man. This is why in this instance at least we have to go back and look at the original context in order to understand Jesus' words. It highlights for us the fact that the Old Testament argument or narrative may be brought into view not merely because it offers some proof or prediction of current or future events. It may also be used – and arguably most often is used – in order to *interpret* these events. In the same way, when Jesus tells his followers that some of them will 'see' the Son of Man coming in his kingdom (Matt. 16:28), he does not mean that they will see in a literal, physical sense a human figure approaching the throne of the Ancient of Days – and certainly not descending to earth from heaven on a cloud. He means that they will meet a future state of affairs that must be understood *in the light of* this symbolic vision.

But we are running ahead of ourselves. The general question to be considered is: How does the language of prophecy and theological reflection that we find in the New Testament – and by which such broad activities as mission are defined – relate to the experiences and expectations of the believing community as it is carried along by the fast-flowing river of history? Or very simply: How does the New Testament *see* its world? We are learning to *imagine* the effect of retelling certain decisive narratives under the concrete and limited circumstances of first-century Judaism. It is an exercise in what we might call *contextual or perspectival narrative realism*.

In this compact saying, then, Jesus evokes the image of the angels of God ascending and descending – like commuters on an escalator – and he attaches it to a quite different story about the Son of Man. In the intersection of these two narratives we find our central contention, which is that *the calling of a people to be a new creation is redefined, but not displaced, by its collision with a story about suffering and vindication.* We will give some thought, first, to the origins of these two stories; then we will see how the pattern is repeated, in rather different terms, in two intersecting arguments about righteousness and faith in Romans.

The promise to Jacob

Nathanael has acclaimed Jesus as Son of God and Israel's king – the two terms are virtually synonymous and are probably meant to recall Psalm 2: the nations oppose YHWH and his anointed king, but today the king has been 'begotten' as YHWH's 'son' and will 'break them with a rod of iron and dash them in pieces like a potter's vessel.'

This is remarkable enough, and we will have more to say about this theme later. But Jesus tells them that they will see something 'greater' than the victory of Israel's king over his enemies: they will see the angels of God ascending and descending not, as we might have expected, above the sleeping form of Jacob but on the Son of Man. So it is not Jacob but the Son of Man who now hears the three-part promise from the Lord standing at the top of the stairway. It is the Son of Man whose descendants will be like the dust of the earth, spreading throughout the land 'to the west and to the east and to the north and to the south,' and through whom 'all the families of the earth will be blessed.' In effect, the promise has been transferred.

We could leave things here and perhaps draw some rather conventional conclusions about the expansion of the church. But I think we need to listen a little more attentively to the reverberations of this promise in the patriarchal narratives. It was originally given, of course, to Abraham, as Isaac reminds Jacob before his departure to Paddan-aram: 'God Almighty bless you and make you fruitful and multiply you, that you may become a company of peoples. May he give the blessing of Abraham to you and to your offspring with you, that you may take possession of the land of your sojournings that God gave to Abraham!' (Gen. 28:3–4). The same three elements are here: the numerical increase of descendants, the expansion throughout the land, and the blessing of God. But we also now hear unmistakable echoes of an earlier narrative about the creation of humankind. When Isaac prays that God will bless Jacob, make him fruitful and multiply him, and that he will take possession of the land, he simply restates the original blessing of Genesis 1:28: 'And God blessed them. And God said to them, "Be fruitful and multiply and fill the earth." ' The formula has been adapted in only one respect: it is not the earth that Jacob's descendants will fill but Canaan, to which he will eventually return following his wanderings (28:15).

By conjuring up for Nathanael, from the depths of Israel's memory, the vision of Jacob's flight of steps touching the heavens, Jesus awakens thoughts of creation, of a new beginning for humanity, of increase and dispersal throughout the earth/land, of blessing, and well-being. In order to understand the significance of this memory for the story about Jesus and the emergence of a community of followers we need to look more closely at the narrative that connects the original blessing with the promise made to the patriarchs.

Abraham and the creational mandate

Having made the man and the woman in his own image, God blesses them and tells them: 'Be fruitful and multiply and fill the earth and subdue it' (1:28). Because they are disobedient and choose to eat of the tree of knowledge of good and evil, the blessing is compromised, if not quite revoked. Adam and Eve are expelled from the benign environment of the garden; they will still multiply and fill the earth, but the woman will suffer pain in childbirth; they will subdue the earth, but the ground is now cursed because of them, and it will be a struggle to sustain life – until eventually they return to the dust from which they were taken.

Following this initial loss of innocence, humankind begins to increase in number and spread across the face of the earth, as was originally intended. But because of the wickedness of people's hearts and their propensity for violence God destroys everything that has become corrupt in a cataclysmic flood, regretting that he ever brought the world into being. The creational impulse to multiply and fill the earth is arrested as life is swept away. We are back at square one. The process must be restarted. So when the waters subside, we hear again the original blessing: 'God blessed Noah and his sons and said to them, "Be fruitful and multiply and fill the earth" ' (9:1). The world is made again. A new expansion begins. The families of Noah's sons become nations, sharing a single language; and they 'spread abroad on the earth after the flood' (10:32 – 11:1).

Unfortunately, they get only as far as a plain in the land of Shinar where they set about building a city with a tower that would reach to the heavens, because they are afraid of being 'dispersed over the face of the whole earth' (11:4). They defy the command to take responsibility for the world and instead seek to construct their own centralized, monolithic, self-aggrandizing environment that will guarantee their security and glory. The Lord's response is to confuse their language, to create misunderstanding and division, and to scatter them 'from there over the face of all the earth' (11:8).

What this sequence of disruptions has shown is that humanity is consistently unwilling to live within the terms of the original blessing – that is, to be a prolific people dispersed throughout the world, responsible managers of the ecosystem of which they are part, sharing a common obedience as a matter both of worship and of justice to the creative God. What we have instead are forcibly scattered nations, isolated from each other linguistically and culturally, ambitious to make a name for themselves by means of their technological ingenuity, and worshiping instead their various substandard deities. Creation has again broken down, this time at a political and cultural level.

It is at this point that God invites Abraham (originally Abram) to be the progenitor of a great nation. He will bless him and make his name great; he will make him fruitful; he will multiply his descendants, making them like the dust of the earth, the stars of heaven; above all, he will give to Abraham and his descendants the land of Canaan, in which they will prosper (cf. Gen. 12:2–3, 7; 13:15–16; 15:5; 17:2–6, 8). The language recalls the blessing of Genesis 1:28, except that the earth has been reduced to the dimensions of the small but fecund land of Canaan. Humanity has failed to fulfill the conditions of the original mandate on a global scale, so Abraham is called to inaugurate a creation in microcosm, a world-within-a-world – a prosperous people in a good land in the midst of the divided and headstrong nations of the earth. It is a response not primarily to the problem of personal sin but to the persistent failure of human society to understand in what way it has been blessed by God. If this is the starting point for understanding the purpose of the church, it suggests that we need to think in terms not of individuals but of *groups* – nations, cultures, communities. The fundamental initiative of God is to choose a 'people for his treasured possession, out of all the peoples who are on the face of the earth' (Deut. 14:2).

The fate of the microcosm

What happens to the creational microcosm? The story is too complex to tell in detail, but it needs to be told at least in a way that does not lose sight of the original calling of the people to be a reinstated creation, dynamically present amidst the nations of the earth.

In the events of the exodus the story of the inauguration of a subset of humanity through Abraham is developed and expanded in a number of important respects. First, the calling of Abraham is overlaid with a narrative about the redemption of the people from slavery in Egypt. It is built into Israel's self-understanding, therefore, from a very early stage that they are always vulnerable in the world and cannot expect to fulfill their purpose apart from the saving intervention of YHWH in some form or other. They are always a new humanity rescued or redeemed from the corruption of the macrocosm, expressed in this case as political oppression; and through storytelling, ritual, and the goading of prophecy they are repeatedly reminded of this.

Secondly, the law is given through Moses as a codification of the obedient trust in the promise that is expressed, for example, in Abraham's willingness to sacrifice the child through whom the promise is supposed to be fulfilled (Gen. 22:16–18; cf. 26:5). If Israel is to prosper in the creational microcosm of Canaan, the people must obey the voice of the Lord their God; they must keep 'his charge, his statutes, his rules, and his commandments always' (Deut. 11:1). If they fail to keep the commandments, if they fail to maintain the spiritual and moral integrity of the community, the outlook will be bleak. They will suffer sickness and drought; their livestock will become barren; their crops will fail; they will be defeated and killed by their enemies; ultimately, they will be driven from the land and exiled among the nations – in short, they will suffer the total collapse of the microcosm (cf. Deut. 28:15–68).

Thirdly, Israel takes possession of the land through conquest. Whatever we may make of the morality of the seizure of Canaan, it is important to observe that it entails fundamentally a decisive and definitive repudiation of idolatry. On the one hand, it is a judgement on and eradication of the idolatry and wickedness of the Canaanites (e.g. Deut. 9:4–5; 12:29–31). On the other, it is accompanied by the command to Israel to abandon the 'gods your fathers served in the region beyond the River, or the gods of the Amorites in whose land you dwell.' The people at this point freely enter into an agreement to serve only YHWH, who 'brought us and our fathers up from the land of Egypt, out of the house of slavery' (Josh. 24:14–18). In other words, it represents a judgement on the idolatrous corruption of the created order and establishes the microcosm *as a sign that YHWH is God of the whole earth.*

Fourthly, as the microcosm evolves, it begins to adopt the characteristics of the surrounding nations. So when the elders of Israel petition Samuel to appoint a king for them, their desire is that 'we also may be like all the nations, and that our king may judge us and go out before us and fight our battles' (1 Sam. 8:20; cf. 9:16; 10:1). They wish to adopt as the template for this authentic humanity the dominant socio-political system of the ancient Near East, not least because they recognize themselves to be in conflict with the nations around them. But the ideal creational *paradigm* remains intact: a people in relationship with the creative God, practicing social justice, and prospering in the land.

Perhaps inevitably, however, this ambitious experiment in the reimagining of creation fails. Israel worships other gods, abandons justice, and as a consequence is defeated in war and removed from the land. Samaria, the capital of the northern kingdom, falls to the Assyrians in 721 BC, following Hoshea's foolhardy mutiny, and the people are deported to Mesopotamia and Media (2 Kgs. 17:4–6). The southern kingdom suffers the same fate not much more than a hundred years later when first Johoikim and later Zedekiah rebel against the Babylonians. The upshot is that Jerusalem and the temple are burned to the ground, the defensive walls of the city are demolished, the leaders of Judah are executed, and most of the population are taken into exile in Babylon, leaving only the poorest of the land to serve as vinedressers and plowmen (25:1–21).

The microcosm has collapsed; and if it is to be restored, if the promise to Abraham is to remain viable, God must act to defeat his enemies, liberate his people from their oppressors, break open the gates of their captivity, and lead them back to the land that was promised to them. A political quandary demands a political solution. This is the 'good news,' the message of hope, that is announced to Zion: 'Your God reigns' (Isa. 52:7). The watchmen of Jerusalem will see the return of the Lord to Zion. He has acted in sight of the nations to save his people and re-establish righteousness and justice (51:4; 52:8–10).

But the foreseen restoration of exiled Israel is *creational* in its scope. The one God, who created the heavens and the earth (45:18; cf. 54:5), will re-establish his place in the midst of his people (cf. Zech. 8:7–8); the city of YHWH will be rebuilt (Isa. 61:4; 62:7). The dispersion of the people from the land will be reversed. The exiles will be brought back from the ends of the earth to form a new righteous community (54:14; 60:21). The landscape will be transformed (41:17–20). Because of the creational promise to Abraham, the waste places of Zion will be made like Eden, 'her desert like the garden of the LORD'

(51:2–3); in place of thorns and briers there will be cypress and myrtle (55:13); and there is the glorious, stomping image of the mountains and hills breaking into singing, the trees of the field clapping their hands in delight at the restoration of God's people (55:12). The population of Jerusalem will be multiplied; they will 'spread abroad to the right and to the left,' in fulfillment of the creational directive; their descendants will 'possess the nations and will people the desolate cities' (54:3).

In sum, the salvation of Israel, exiled from a land wasted by war and neglect, oppressed by its enemies, is conceived by Isaiah as a recovery of the creational vision: 'For behold, I create new heavens and a new earth, and the former things shall not be remembered or come into mind' (65:17). This is metaphorical language. It is a statement, on the one hand, that the sin that resulted in the judgement of the exile will be remembered no more and, on the other, that this is a new beginning for a people called originally to be an authentic humanity, a creational microcosm, a world-within-a-world. There is an idyllic aspect to the vision that will always feed a longing for the perfect: there will no longer be heard the cries of distress of a ravaged population; their houses and crops will not be plundered by invaders; they will not bear children only for them to be killed in the calamity of war (65:19–23). But we are still in the mundane order of things. The people will be blessed, as God promised to bless Abraham, as he once blessed Adam and Eve, but death and sin have not been abolished: 'the young man shall die a hundred years old, and the sinner a hundred years old shall be accursed' (65:20). We should also note that the famous cessation of hostilities in the animal kingdom does not represent a universal transformation of creation. It is limited to the land and to God's holy mountain; it is symbolic of Israel's prosperity: the wolf will not devour their sheep, the lion will not kill their oxen, farmers will not be bitten by snakes as they work in the fields (65:25).

The remaining element to add to this picture of the restoration of exiled Israel as a creation in miniature is its situation among the nations. Attracted like moths to the light of what God has done for his people, the nations will become willing participants in the restoration of ruined Jerusalem: they will escort the captives home; they will bring tribute of gold, silver, and frankincense; they will build up the walls; timber from Lebanon will be used to adorn the temple (60:13–14; cf. 61:5 – 62:3). Here is the 'missional' pattern of the good news to exiled Israel: YHWH saves his people from the ruin of their world, and this dramatic act of political-religious salvation will make such an impression on the nations that they will be drawn into the event, not as spectators only but as actors. The expectation is again that Israel will become an authentic humanity, modelling righteousness and justice, the creative God resident in glory in its midst – a sign to the world that God has remained faithful to his promise to bless the seed of Abraham (61:9).

In the midst of this narrative of creational renewal in Isaiah, however, we come across a remarkable, perhaps even incongruous, story about suffering and death – the story of a righteous servant who spoke what he heard from God, who was not rebellious, who was beaten and humiliated (50:4–6), who was 'despised and rejected by men,' who suffered hurt and in the end death because of the transgressions of the people of Jerusalem. Of course, we immediately think 'Jesus.' But the route by which we arrive at that identification is not a straightforward one; and what we actually find when we get there may not be quite what we imagined.

The story of the Son of Man

Jesus' response to Nathanael connects two Old Testament narratives. The first is the story of the repeated promise to Jacob that creation will be restarted in microcosm through his descendants. The second is the story – no less intriguing – of the 'Son of Man.' We are so accustomed to reading this phrase in the Gospels as a title for Jesus that we easily miss the narrative significance that it draws from Daniel 7 – 12. 'Son of Man' is not a title: it is a story. The apocalyptic drama that unfolds in these chapters is lurid and perplexing but it is not incomprehensible and is crucial for understanding how the two narratives intersect.

Daniel 7 describes a symbolic judgement scene. Four composite mythical beasts emerge from a troubled sea. The fourth is more terrible than the others: 'It had great iron teeth; it devoured and broke in pieces and stamped what was left with its feet.' On its head are ten horns; and Daniel sees another little horn appear, with 'eyes like the eyes of a man, and a mouth speaking great things' (Dan. 7:7–8). At this point thrones are set up, the Ancient of Days takes his seat, and the court sits in judgement over the beasts. It is important to see that in the vision this takes place *on earth*: there would have been no need to set up a throne for God in heaven, certainly not a throne with wheels (7:9); and the little horn, which represents an earthly king, is ranting in the presence of the court. The fourth beast is killed and its body destroyed, burned with fire. The other three beasts are allowed to live, but 'dominion' or 'authority' is taken from them. Then Daniel sees another vision in the night – not a beast this time but a human figure, one like a son of man, coming with the clouds of heaven to be presented before the Ancient of Days. He is given 'dominion and glory and a kingdom, that all peoples, nations, and languages should serve him; his dominion is an everlasting dominion, which shall not pass away, and his kingdom one that shall not be destroyed' (7:14).

What follows in the second half of the chapter is an inter-pretation of this drama. Daniel asks one of the court attendants what these alarming visions signify. He is told that the four beasts are kings or kingdoms. The little horn on the head of the fourth beast, which so fascinates and appals him, is an arrogant and impious king who will make war against the saints of the Most High, seeking to abolish their ancient customs and loyalties. But although they will be given into his hand for a while, the king will be judged, his dominion will be taken away, and he will be destroyed. Whereas in the vision it is the 'son of man' figure who receives the kingdom, in the interpretation 'the kingdom and the dominion and the greatness of the kingdoms under the whole heaven shall be given to the people of the saints of the Most High' (7:27). It is clear that just as the beasts are symbolic representations not of individuals but of kingdoms (the fourth beast is the Macedonian empire of Alexander the

Great), so the figure in human form represents a group – the saints of the Most High.

The drama of Daniel 7, however, needs to be read as the climax to a more complex narrative about the *forgiveness of Israel* that is told in chapter 9. Daniel has read in Jeremiah that seventy years must pass 'before the end of the desolations of Jerusalem' (9:2). He confesses the sins of Israel, admits that YHWH has been righteous (that is, justified) in his actions, and prays for forgiveness, for the anger and wrath of the Lord to be turned away from Jerusalem. At this point the 'man Gabriel' appears to him to give 'insight and understanding' (9:22). He reinterprets Jeremiah's seventy years as, in effect, 'seventy weeks of years' or 490 years, and outlines the events that will take place before the anger of God toward Israel is brought to an end and an 'everlasting righteousness' is introduced. After seven weeks of years an anointed prince will rebuild Jerusalem following its destruction by the Babylonians. The next sixty-two weeks will be a 'troubled time' for the city, culminating in the cutting off of an anointed one and the destruction of the city and the sanctuary by the 'people of the prince who is to come' (9:25–26). During the final week this prince will 'make a strong covenant with many,' and for half of the week 'he shall put an end to sacrifice and offering.' The 'abomination of desolations' will appear in the temple, but eventually the desolation will be brought to an end (9:27 LXX).[1]

The events of this last week are 'foretold' in greater detail in Daniel 11:29 – 12:4. The king will 'take action against the holy covenant'; he will enter into an alliance with apostate Jews who forsake the covenant; his forces will profane the temple, take away the regular burnt offering, and set up the abomination that makes desolate; Jews who are wise, who know their God, who are faithful to the traditions of their ancestors, will be subjected to sword, flame, captivity, and plunder; the king will elevate himself above every god and will 'speak astonishing things' against the God of Israel; he will prosper until the 'indignation is accomplished'; there will be a period of unprecedented suffering for the Jews, but in the end those who are faithful will be delivered and will receive a kingdom. We are back at the original judgement scene and the verdict given in favor of the saints of the Most High, who are to 'possess the kingdom.'

This story about the intrusion of a hostile pagan power, a crisis of the covenant, and a resulting time of great affliction provides a multifaceted, multilayered eschatological paradigm. It originally foretold or described the impact that the aggressive Hellenizing interference of the Syrian king Antiochus IV, known as Epiphanes, would have on the people of the covenant. But Jesus clearly sees in it the potential to give expression to a much greater crisis that will soon engulf Israel.

John's Gospel lacks the hallmark apocalyptic vision of one like a son of man coming with the clouds of heaven that is found in the Synoptic Gospels. But the connection between Jesus' use of the phrase and Daniel's eschatological drama is not difficult to discern beneath the layers of Johannine theology. Just as Daniel's symbolic human figure represents the community of the righteous in Israel that suffers under pagan oppression, the 'Son of Man,' Jesus says, will be lifted up from the earth on a Roman cross (John 12:32–33; cf. 3:14; 8:28). Just as Daniel's Son of Man is given authority to rule over the nations, so Jesus is given 'authority to execute judgment, because he is the Son of Man' (Dan. 7:14 LXX; John 5:27; cf. 9:35–39). This judgement is then described in language taken from Daniel 12:2: 'an hour is coming when all who are in the tombs will hear his voice and come out, those who have done good to the resurrection of life, and those who have done evil to the resurrection of judgement' (John 5:28–29). This is the judgement on Israel that will finally bring to an end the alienation of the exiled people and establish righteousness. Just as Daniel's Son of Man is given 'glory,' when Judas leaves the upper room to betray him, Jesus declares, 'Now is the Son of Man glorified' (John 13:31).

What Nathanael and others will 'see,' therefore, is the fusion of two nocturnal narratives, two bedtime stories: Jacob's dream of a fruitful new humanity, multiplying and filling the land of Canaan, and Daniel's vision in the night of a community that will receive 'dominion and glory and a kingdom.' Jesus is Jacob hearing again an ancient promise, but he identifies himself at the same time with the symbolic figure in Daniel 7 who is seen coming on the clouds of heaven, approaching the judgement seat of the Ancient of Days. Just as Jacob will be the progenitor of a nation, the 'one like a son of man' that Daniel sees represents, according to the angel's interpretation, the righteous in Israel against whom the little horn on the head of the fourth beast makes war. If the creation story is to be retold here, it will be as part of a dark apocalyptic drama about a people that suffers and is eventually vindicated before the throne of God.

Approaching the intersection

The argument of this book will be that the basic impulse for mission comes from the first of these two stories. The New Testament, however, is preoccupied with the second. The challenge we face is to understand how they intersect. We will approach it from two directions. We will explore the narrative about Jesus within the historical framework of the Gospels and the book of Acts. But the narrative intersection is also apparent in Paul's letter to the Romans. The point can be illustrated rather neatly. Two gnomic statements about righteousness and faith underpin Paul's argument in Romans: 'Abraham had faith in God, and it was counted to him as righteousness' (Rom. 4:3, my translation; cf. 4:9, 22; Gal. 3:6); and 'The righteous shall live by faith' (Rom. 1:17; cf. Gal. 3:11). Both are quotations from the Old Testament; both stand for extensive narratives.

The first comes from Genesis 15:6. When Abraham complains to God that he has no heir and that, as things stand, at his death everything will go to an obscure member of his household, he is assured that he will have a son of his own and that his descendants will be like the stars of heaven in number. Abraham *believes the promise,* and this belief or trust or faith is counted to him as righteousness. He is then told that even though his descendants will find themselves enslaved and afflicted 'in a land that is not theirs' for four hundred years, God will bring judgement upon that nation (that is, Egypt) and the people will eventually return to the land promised to them. This paradigmatic link between faith and righteousness is a crucial element in Paul's argument in Romans 4 about the justification of a people by faith or faithfulness. To those who believe or trust or have faith in the God who raised Jesus from the dead it will be counted as righteousness.

The second statement comes from Habakkuk 2:4. The prophet, writing around 600 BC, is distressed by the level of violence and injustice that he sees in Israel, and he calls out to God: 'O LORD, how long shall I cry for help, and you will not hear? Or cry to you "Violence!" and you will not save?' He is told to look among the nations because God is about to raise up the Chaldeans – 'that bitter and hasty nation, who march through the breadth of the earth, to seize dwellings not their own.' They will attack the land of Israel, overcome its fortresses and take the people captive, because 'the law is paralyzed, and justice never goes forth . . . the wicked surround the righteous; so justice goes forth perverted' (Hab. 1:2–4). The vision may seem slow in coming, but sooner or later the horrors of military invasion will descend upon Israel, leading to death, destruction, and deportation. This is geopolitics as usual in the ancient Near-East, but within the story that Israel told about itself it has to be interpreted as God's judgement on an unfaithful and unjust people. Here we come to the crucial dilemma. Not all in Israel are wicked, so what will become of the *righteous* – the poor, the afflicted, the victims of oppression and violence? The righteous will live, Habakkuk says, by virtue of their faithfulness, their steadfast trust in God (2:4).

These two rather similar statements arise out of two quite different stories. One has to do with God calling a people into existence through a promise to Abraham that his descendants will become a nation and inherit the land of Canaan. Abraham *believes* this promise and it is counted to him as *righteousness*. The other connects belief and righteousness under circumstances of stress and conflict: when the people of the promise face destruction because of their wickedness, those who are righteous, who do not deserve to be destroyed, will live by their faith because they trust God enough not to shrink back (cf. Hab. 2:4 LXX; Heb. 10:38), enough to remain loyal and steadfast. This is the backdrop to the story of Jesus, who takes upon himself the role of the Son of Man who will suffer for the sake of the promise that was repeated to Jacob as he slept under a starry sky.

3

Down the Rabbit Hole: The Beginning of the Gospel of Jesus Christ

In Lewis Carroll's *Alice in Wonderland*, when Alice finally reached the bottom of the rabbit hole, she found herself in a 'long, low hall, which was lit up by a row of lamps hanging from the roof.' All the doors around the hall were locked, but there was a small golden key on a glass table with which she was able to open a little door, about fifteen inches high, hidden behind a curtain. The door led into a small passage, 'not much larger than a rat-hole,' at the end of which she could see a beautiful garden with beds of bright flowers and cool fountains. But she was unable to get her head through the doorway – and even if she had succeeded, it would have been useless without the rest of her body. 'Oh, how I wish I could shut up like a telescope!' Alice lamented. 'I think I could, if I only knew how to begin.'

She returned to the glass table and this time found on it a small bottle with a label attached that read 'Drink me.' Having sensibly checked to see whether the bottle was marked 'poison,' she drank its contents, and found herself shrinking to a size that would comfortably fit through the door.

The fact that Alice had inadvertently left the golden key out of reach on the glass table, and that it would be some time – and some odd adventures – before she could get through the door into the mysterious garden, is a warning to us that the mental exercise on which we have embarked is not at all an easy one. We need to imagine that the world of the New Testament is to be found down a deep rabbit hole and through a door that our large modern heads cannot enter. We need to take the risk of drinking a strangely intoxicating, disorienting potion that will shrink our minds to the dimensions of an ancient, constricted, and in many respects disturbing worldview.

In this chapter we enter that world, at the beginning of the story about Jesus of Nazareth, with the broad missional question in mind: How in the mind of God is the church intended to relate to the nations and cultures of the world? What we are seeking to understand is the role that Jesus plays, not in the popular abstraction, the emaciated, ahistorical myth of personal salvation that is the legacy of the modern enculturation of Christian faith, but in the complex story that the Bible tells about the world-within-a-world that becomes the nation of Israel and then becomes something else. In view of this it may seem a little ironic that we begin with the birth narratives. Too often these familiar stories have been ridiculed or revered as the product of pious fancy. They are much more serious than that. In a quite relevant and arguably quite realistic manner they address the historical condition of first-century Israel and give expression to the hope of national deliverance that for one Jewish sect came to be focused in Jesus of Nazareth. We will then look at the early events of his recorded career as an eschatological agitator: his baptism in the Jordan, the testing of his calling in the wilderness, and the initial announcement to Israel about the coming of the reign of God.

He will save his people from their sins

Mary is inexplicably pregnant. Joseph is about to break off the engagement quietly, but an angel of the Lord intervenes in a dream and explains to him that the child conceived in her is of the Holy Spirit. Joseph is to name the boy Jesus, for he will 'save his people from their sins' (Matt. 1:21). Almost every word in this simple statement is more peculiar than we might think. Why? Because we are accustomed to reading definitive theological pronouncements such as this from the high walls of an intellectual fortress built by Christendom. From this elevated position it has always seemed that the angel must be saying something about the salvation of all humanity from a condition of personal sinfulness. But the fortress is being demolished, and everything looks rather different now that we stand, in a state of some shock, amid its ruins.

First, the innocuous pronoun 'his' fixes the scope of the 'salvation' that is announced by the angel: it is not the whole world but Jesus' *own people* that will be saved. Likewise, when the angel announces to the shepherds 'good news of a great joy that will be for all the people,' he means all the people *of Israel*, not all humankind (Luke 2:10). It is the same 'people' to which Zechariah refers when he prophesies about the redemption of Israel (Luke 1:68, 77). The restriction is reinforced in the birth narratives by the repeated assertion that Jesus will be king *of the Jews*. The stargazers from the East ask, 'Where is he who has been born *king of the Jews*?' (Matt. 2:2). The chief priests and scribes inform Herod that according to the prophet the Christ will come from Bethlehem – 'a ruler who will govern *my people Israel*' (Matt. 2:6; cf. Mic. 5:2) at a time when the nations are assembled against Jerusalem, when siege is laid against the city, and 'with a rod they strike the judge of Israel on the cheek' (Mic. 4:11; 5:1). We are meant to pick up these overtones of political crisis. Mary is told that Jesus 'will reign *over the house of Jacob* for ever' (Luke 1:33). There is a shrunken, down-the-rabbit-hole perspective on things here that we need to grasp. This is not the transcendent, universal *cosmocrator* of later faith: it is a child who will become – improbably – the 'king' of a small cantankerous Middle Eastern nation currently under Roman occupation.

When Simeon sees the baby being carried into the temple, he approaches the family, takes Jesus in his arms and blesses God because in his old age, after so many years looking for 'the consolation of Israel,' he has seen the salvation that God has 'prepared in the presence of all peoples, a light for revelation to the Gentiles, and for glory to your people Israel' (Luke 2:25–32). This reference to the nations needs to be deciphered carefully. It is still Israel that will be *saved*, not the world; but the salvation of Israel will consequently be 'a light for revelation to the Gentiles.'

In order to understand this phrase, which must be of some importance for a biblical theory of mission, we need to attend to certain precise Old Testament echoes. Psalm 98:1–3 speaks of the salvation of Israel that God has 'made known'; his righteousness has been 'revealed . . . in the sight of the nations.' 'All the ends of the earth have seen the salvation of our God.' In Isaiah the servant of the Lord will bring about the restoration of Israel and in the process will be 'a light for the nations' (Isa. 49:6; cf. 42:6). He will release the prisoners from darkness (49:6; cf. 42:7; 61:1), he will open the eyes of blind Israel (42:7; cf. 6:10; 29:9, 18; 35:5; 42:16, 18, 19; 43:8; 56:10; 59:10); he will 'bring back the preserved of Israel' (49:6). But this salvation will have an impact on the nations: they will see what God has done for his people (52:10), they will see the character of his righteousness and justice, they will acknowledge his power and glory (49:7), they will be instrumental in bringing back the scattered Jews to Zion (49:22; 60:4), they will travel to see the 'light' of Israel, bringing tribute and praise (60:1–14), they will recognize the people of Israel as 'priests of the LORD . . . ministers of our God' (61:6), they will see the righteousness and glory of Israel (62:2).

The point of all this is that when God acts sovereignly to save his covenant people, it will not be in covert, hugger-mugger fashion – an obscure shift in national fortunes that no one really notices. When God comes to judge the earth, to put things right, to restore righteousness and justice, it will happen in full view of the nations – and they will be astonished at what has happened. They will come, as the Persian astrologers came, to prostrate themselves before, and offer tribute to, Israel's newborn king.

Secondly, it is a *people* that will be saved. Although there is no 'people' without individuals, just as there is no forest without trees or swarm without bees, what is in view here is the *political survival of a nation*, not a universalized personal salvation. When people choose to follow Jesus in the Gospels, they do so as representatives of Israel, not as samples from the whole of humanity.

Thirdly, Israel's 'sins' must be understood historically. Tightly coiled up in this small but not so innocuous word, like a DNA molecule in a chromosome, is a long story about a nation that consistently failed to live up to its own ideals and suffered the consequences of failure. It is a story of entrenched idolatry and injustice, of spiritual obstinacy, of habitual rebellion against God, resulting in devastation, exile from the land, and subjection to foreign powers. It is told in Psalm 106; Stephen tells it in Acts 7. We will not understand the Gospels properly if we insist on reading 'sins' as a reference essentially to a generalized human condition. We must think in terms of patterns of national behavior that are at odds with Israel's ideal character and purpose.

The point is underlined by Matthew's allusion to the name Immanuel: ' "Behold, the virgin shall conceive and bear a son, and they shall call his name Immanuel" (which means, God with us)' (Matt. 1:23; cf. Isa. 7:14). How does this work? Isaiah addresses a political crisis faced by King Ahaz of Judah around 735 BC. The kings of Syria and Samaria (that is, the northern kingdom of Israel) have joined forces to wage war against Jerusalem. Isaiah assures the distrustful Ahaz that nothing will come of this and offers him a sign from the Lord: a young woman will conceive and give birth to a son, who will be given the name 'Immanuel.' The child does not do anything: he does not grow up to be a saviour or king or messiah. He is simply a sign, by virtue of his birth and his name, that within a few years God will intervene to dramatic effect: 'The LORD will bring upon you and upon your people and upon your father's house such days as have not come since the day that Ephraim departed from Judah – the king of Assyria' (Isa. 7:17). The Assyrian invasion, like a great river, will bring devastation upon Syria and Samaria, the two nations that threatened Judah. But because Judah did not trust God during this crisis, the river will not stop here but 'will sweep on into Judah, it will overflow and pass on, reaching even to the neck, and its outspread wings will fill the breadth of your land, O Immanuel' (8:8). The fact that 'God is with us' is an assurance that when Jerusalem faces military disaster, God will not allow his people to be completely overwhelmed (8:9–10). So if 'Immanuel' means salvation for Israel, it is not in any harmless sense. The remarkable circumstances of Jesus' birth are a sign that God will be present in Israel not to comfort but to *confront* a people who have no fear of the Lord.

Finally, it is from this state of alienation from the God of its fathers, experienced in the form of political oppression, that Israel needs to be *saved*. There is nothing metaphorical about Zechariah's prophecy following the birth of John. Redemption for Israel, during the reign of the emperor Augustus, when Quirinius is governor of Syria, means deliverance 'from our enemies and from the hand of all who hate us' so that the people may serve God without the fear that characterizes a state of subjugation – fear of harassment, brutality, tyranny, and sacrilege (Luke 1:71, cf. 1:74). Zechariah is looking for régime change. Those to whom the aged prophetess Anna spoke, who 'were waiting for the redemption of Jerusalem' (Luke 2:38), were not hoping for the salvation of their souls but longed to see 'the City of the LORD, the Zion of the Holy One of Israel' (Isa. 60:14) liberated from pagan rule. How this deliverance was to come about was another matter, but it was not to be less than *the rescue of a people from a political condition* – a state of subjugation because of sin that was fundamentally at odds with the calling to be God's 'treasured possession among all peoples' (Exod. 19:5).

The beloved Son

The story of Jesus' baptism strikes the same resonant nationalist chords. Emerging from the water he sees the heavens opened and, as the Spirit of God comes to rest upon him in the form of a dove, a voice from heaven is heard: 'You are my beloved Son; with you I am well pleased' (Mark 1:11; cf. Matt. 3:17); or as an alternative reading of Luke 3:22 has it: 'You are my beloved Son; today I have begotten you.' The announcement pulls two important threads from the Old Testament and weaves them into the baptism story.

The first is the statement made by YHWH to Israel's king in Psalm 2:7: 'You are my Son; today I have begotten you.' The psalm speaks of the antagonism of the nations toward the Lord and his anointed king. In response to the political crisis YHWH, who holds the rulers of the world in derision, makes Israel's king a 'son,' gives birth to him at that moment – the point of the metaphor being that as a son *he will receive the nations as an inheritance*; the ends of the earth will be his possession (Ps. 2:8). This is not, however, an image of the salvation of the nations; it is an image of judgement, conquest, or rule. Israel's king, having been born today as YHWH's son, will break the nations with a rod of iron and smash them like a clay pot (2:9). The political theme cannot be marginalized simply because we have a modern preference for more spiritualized forms of belief. We will find ourselves coming back to it repeatedly.

The second passage is Isaiah 42:1: 'Behold my servant, whom I uphold, my chosen, in whom my soul delights; I have put my Spirit upon him; he will bring forth justice to the nations.' The son who is given the nations as an inheritance is also the beloved servant chosen by YHWH and given the Holy Spirit in order to establish justice in the earth (42:1–4). Again, we should assume that the allusion is meant to place Jesus' baptism in a narrative about Israel and retell it for a new but analogous set of circumstances. The story needs to be carefully disentangled from the exuberant, dense, and multilayered poetry of Isaiah 40 – 55.

1. The servant described by Isaiah, upon whom God puts his Spirit, is Jacob, the 'offspring of Abraham,' the 'men of Israel' whom God redeems (41:8, 14; cf. 44:3). If Jesus is to be understood at this point as the fulfillment of Isaiah's vision of the servant, it is not because Isaiah speaks of a future individual but because Jesus enacts *Israel's story* – or more exactly, anticipates the story of the community through which the future of the people of God will be vouchsafed.

2. The account of the servant's calling presupposes the historical setting of Israel in exile as a consequence of sin. The servant in whom YHWH delights is also blind and deaf, refusing to walk in the ways of the Lord, wearying him with their iniquities (42:18–20, 24; 43:24; 48:1–11). So God delivered 'Jacob to utter destruction and Israel to reviling' (43:28; 51:17). But then we also hear the ringing announcement that Jerusalem's warfare is ended, that her iniquity is pardoned (40:2–5; 43:25). YHWH is doing something fundamentally

new in Israel (42:9; 43:18–19; 48:6). He is coming to redeem and renew his people (44:22–23; 46:13; 48:20; 49:13; 51:3); he will send Cyrus to break open the doors of Babylon so that Israel may go free (45:1–2; cf. 43:14; 48:14); he will bring them back from their exile at the ends of the earth (41:9; 43:5–7; 45:13; 49:22; 51:11); he will rebuild Jerusalem and its temple (44:26, 28); he will make an everlasting covenant with them (54:10; 55:3); he will defeat their enemies (41:11; 42:13; 49:26; 51:22–23).

3. The salvation of Israel is a sign that YHWH reigns. The Lord has acted sovereignly before the nations in redeeming Jerusalem, so that 'all the ends of the earth shall see the salvation of our God' (52:9–10). His judgement on Israel's behalf will go out and shine as a light in the midst of the nations, his arm will overrule the peoples, so that Israel may be saved and brought back to Jerusalem (51:4–6, 11). This is the coming of the kingdom of God: an act of rescue and vindication, a concrete demonstration in the arena of Middle Eastern political-religious rivalry of the fact that Israel's god is not powerless, not inferior to the gods of Israel's enemies. Again, the point to keep in mind is that the situation we encounter in the Gospels is not so different to this; the rhetoric works in pretty much the same way.

4. The story is set against the backdrop of the Creator God's dispute with the nations who practice idolatry (40:12–26; 41:1–7; 42:17; 43:10–13; 44:6–20; 45:20–23) and the proclamation that there is no other god besides YHWH, 'a righteous God and a Saviour' (45:21). Only YHWH can save the nations from destruction – their gods are powerless to protect them; those who survive will recognize the righteousness and strength of the God of Israel (45:14–25). But this salvation is peripheral to the salvation of Israel. Judgement on Babylon is an aspect of the salvation of Israel (47:5–7).

5. The servant will suffer because of his obedience in speaking God's word to Israel: 'I gave my back to those who strike, and

my cheeks to those who pull out the beard; I hid not my face from disgrace and spitting' (50:6). But he knows that he shall not be put to shame, that he 'who vindicates me is near' (50:7–8). His appearance will be marred, he will be despised by the nations, because he shares in the judgement that has come upon Israel because of sin (52:14 – 53:9). But through the suffering the servant, who we must remember is not in any simple sense an individual, will become an offering for sin; by his knowledge he will 'make many to be accounted righteous'; he will bear the sin of many and make intercession for the transgressors (53:10–12).

6. Finally, the servant will fulfill the purposes of YHWH in the earth because he will have the Spirit of God (42:1; 44:3; cf. 61:1). In the first place, he will bring salvation to Israel: he will open the eyes of the blind, he will liberate people from the darkness of their imprisonment (42:7; 49:9; cf. 61:1); he will be a 'covenant to the people' (42:6; 49:8); he will be the means by which God's salvation will reach even to Israel scattered throughout the nations, to the end of the earth (49:6; cf. Deut. 28:64; Isa. 48:20; 62:11). It is always, therefore, *Israel* that is saved, not the Gentiles, though foreigners will 'join themselves to the LORD, to minister to him, to love the name of the LORD, and to be his servants' (56:6) and the nations that once oppressed Israel will serve it (60:10; 61:5–6). This far-reaching act of national salvation will be a sign to the nations that YHWH is the true God, that he reigns, that he is not geopolitically ineffectual, that he has brought about the remarkable transformation of a rebellious people so that they have become a locus of justice and righteousness in the world (42:1–4, 10–25). The servant Jacob will bear witness to the fact that there is no savior but YHWH (43:10–12), no other lord but YHWH (45:6).

The story of the servant, therefore, speaks of a prophetic figure, formed from the womb (cf. Jer. 1:5), who speaks obediently even when he is insulted and beaten (Isa. 50:5–6), who cannot escape the suffering that comes with judgement on Israel, who is also a community and in some sense Israel itself, through whom God will redeem his people and demonstrate his righteousness and strength in the world. In this way 'justice' is restored: the oppression of the people by the nations is brought to an end.

The testing in the wilderness

If the events of Jesus' baptism identify him, first, as the 'son' through whom God will reign over his people in the midst of hostile nations and, secondly, as the servant through whom the justice of God will be demonstrated in the world, what follows is a severe testing of that vocation (Matt. 4:1–11; Mark 1:12–13; Luke 4:1–13). Jesus has become in his own mind the servant Jacob through whom God will restore his people, overcoming the powers, political and otherwise, by which the nation is oppressed. So driven by the Spirit of God he starts to re-enact – we may imagine quite deliberately – the story of Israel's journey toward the fulfillment of the creational impulse in the land. He goes from the water into the wilderness, just as Israel had done, and is pushed to the limits of physical and spiritual endurance. At the end of forty days Satan, Israel's accuser, works his way into his mind. 'If you are the Son of God,' he insinuates, then turn these stones into bread, or throw yourself down from the pinnacle of the temple – let's see if God will send his angels to bear you up. If you are Israel's king, assured of sovereignty amidst the nations that oppose you, if you are the servant Jacob, if you are Israel, the son whom God called out of Egypt (cf. Hos. 11:1) . . . If you think you can really change things . . . Satan challenges this astonishing self-consciousness. Jesus responds by quoting texts from Moses' instructions to Israel as the people got ready, after forty years of wandering, to cross over into the land that YHWH had promised to Abraham (Deut. 8:3; 6:13, 16). This is not an accident. If Israel is again to make the transition from oppression to freedom in God's created space, the people must relearn obedience.

The reign of God is at hand

The beginning of the gospel is the simple announcement: 'Repent, for the kingdom of God is at hand.' As with the angel's words to Joseph, the statement must not be loaded with generalized theological meaning to the point that the narrative substructure collapses under the weight. The message is addressed to the people of Jerusalem, Judea and Galilee; it has to do with the future of occupied Israel; and it speaks of something that will happen soon.

The announcement is heard first from John the son of Zechariah (Matt. 3:2). His function as a prophet is encoded in two Old Testament texts that speak of a 'messenger' who will prepare a way for the Lord, which Mark combines into a single quotation (Mark 1:2–3; cf. Matt. 3:3; 11:10; Luke 7:27; cf. 1:17, 76).

The first passage is Isaiah's description of a voice crying in the wilderness, challenging Israel to make the paths of the Lord straight in advance of his coming (Isa. 40:3). A movement of repentance will prepare the way for an act of salvation that will be seen by the whole world: 'the glory of the LORD shall be revealed, and all flesh shall see it together, for the mouth of the LORD has spoken' (Isa. 40:5). It is the same argument – and the same missional paradigm – that we found in the accounts of Jesus' birth: what God will do in Israel at this juncture will be *seen* by the whole world.

But what is it that he will do in Israel? The voice that is heard in Isaiah comes in response to words of comfort: 'Speak tenderly to Jerusalem, and cry to her that her warfare is ended, that her iniquity is pardoned, that she has received from the LORD's hand double for all her sins' (Isa. 40:2). Isaiah had in mind the Babylonian captivity, but the cry echoes off the canyon wall of history and is heard again centuries later by a people still captive, still oppressed, still alienated from God by their iniquity. If the reign of God is at hand, it will entail the ending of punishment and the forgiveness of Israel's sins.

The second passage is Malachi 3:1. The prophet has complained bitterly about the spiritual and moral failings of the people: the priests offer polluted sacrifices in the temple (1:6–14); the people have worshiped foreign gods (2:11); there is widespread marital breakdown (2:14–16) – and God is getting sick and tired of it (2:17). So he will send a messenger – a prophet like Elijah – to prepare the way for the sudden coming of the Lord to his temple (3:1; cf. 4:5; Matt. 11:14; 17:12; Mark

9:12–13; Luke 1:17). But the Day of the Lord that Malachi imagines is, in the first place, a day of judgement. The Lord will come like a 'refiner's fire' to purify a corrupt priesthood (Mal. 3:3–4). It will be a day of judgement 'against the sorcerers, against the adulterers, against those who swear falsely, against those who oppress the hired worker in his wages, the widow and the fatherless, against those who thrust aside the sojourner' (3:5), a day that will burn up the arrogant and evildoers like stubble in an oven (4:1).

The call to repentance, therefore, that we hear from John is motivated by his conviction that judgement in the form of political disaster is imminent (Matt. 3:7–12; Luke 3:7–17): the Pharisees and Sadducees who come to him are like snakes fleeing from a burning field; the ax is laid to the root of the trees and every tree that does not bear good fruit will be cut down; and the one who comes after him will baptize Israel with the Holy Spirit but also with fire – the chaff from his threshing floor will be burnt with 'unquenchable fire.' This last phrase evokes the grisly description in Isaiah 66:24 of Jerusalem's dead who rebelled against God, whose corpses are consumed by worms that will not die and by a fire that will not be quenched, an 'abhorrence' to all who look upon them. The coming of the reign of God, therefore, will be a double-edged intervention. There is the tantalizing prospect of forgiveness, the hope that the long story of rebellion and punishment will be brought to an end, that a renewed and righteous family of Abraham will emerge (cf. Matt. 3:9; Luke 3:8). But this does not alter the fact that sooner or later the fire of God's wrath will consume Jerusalem and Judea and unrepentant Israel will be ruined.

Your kingdom come . . .

Following the arrest of John, Jesus withdraws to Galilee and sets about preaching the same message: 'Repent, for the kingdom of heaven is at hand' (Matt. 4:12–17; cf. Mark 1:14–15). Two issues need to be addressed regarding the frame of reference of this statement.

First, the announcement is made to Israel and concerns Israel. What Jesus foresees is not a universal reign of God but a dramatic intervention by Israel's true ruler to transform the political-religious condition of his people. It is the same manner of 'good news' that is announced in Isaiah 40:9–10: Jerusalem is the 'herald of good news' who proclaims to the cities of Judah, 'Behold, the Lord GOD comes with might, and his arm rules for him; behold, his reward is with him, and his recompense before him.' Israel's exile is over; Jerusalem's warfare is ended, her iniquity is pardoned, she has received from the Lord's hand double for all her sins (Isa. 40:2). It is the announcement to the 'captive daughter of Zion' that 'Your God reigns,' that he will comfort his people, that he will redeem Jerusalem, that he will return to Zion (Isa. 52:2, 7–8).

For Luke the content of Jesus' preaching about the good news of the kingdom of God is exemplified in his reading from Isaiah 61 in the synagogue in Nazareth (Luke 4:16–21). Jesus assumes the role of an anointed prophet who proclaims hope to oppressed Israel, the defeat of its enemies, and the restoration of devastated Zion. When the disciples of John the Baptist come to him and ask whether he is 'the one who is to come,' Jesus invokes the passage again: 'the blind receive their sight and the lame walk, lepers are cleansed and the deaf hear, and the dead are raised up, and the poor have good news preached to them' (Matt. 11:4–5; cf. Luke 7:22). These 'poor' are not the general destitute of the world; they are, as we shall see later when we come to the beatitudes, specifically those who are afflicted because Israel stands under the heavy judgement of God. The healing of the sick which invariably accompanies the announcement of the good news to oppressed Israel (cf. Matt. 4:23; Mark 1:39) is a sign that at the frayed edges at least Israel is being forgiven. Again, more on this later.

Secondly, the coming of the reign of God is *a future but not a futuristic event:* it does not lie beyond the horizon of people's imaginations and hopes. John calls the inhabitants of Jerusalem and Judea to repent because the kingdom of God is at hand, it has come near: the ax is already laid to the root of the trees (Matt. 3:2, 10). They represent the generation that will experience this decisive and devastating intervention in the affairs of the nation. The same sense of historical urgency attends Jesus' preaching of the good news (Matt. 4:17; Mark 1:15) and the mission he entrusts to his disciples: the reign of God is *at hand* (Matt. 10:5–7; Luke 10:9–11). Behind the Spartan thought are texts such as Isaiah 46:12–13, addressed to the 'transgressors' of Israel (46:8): 'Listen to me, you stubborn of heart, you who are far from righteousness: I bring near my righteousness; *it is not far off, and my salvation will not delay;* I will put salvation in Zion, for Israel my glory' (emphasis added; cf. Isa. 56:1). The coming of the kingdom of God is the transformation of Israel's political-religious condition in the not too distant future.

The sense of imminence is pervasive. The law and commandments will still be operative when the kingdom of God comes (Matt. 5:18–19). Jesus' statement that the law will remain in force 'until heaven and earth pass away . . . until all is accomplished' should be read against the background of poetic passages in Isaiah that contrast God's salvation of Israel with the dissolution of the old heavens and earth. The 'heavens vanish like smoke, the earth will wear out like a garment,' but God's salvation, his deliverance of his people from the consequences of their rebellion, will be forever, will endure to all generations (Isa. 51:6–8). The restoration of Jerusalem will be like the creation of new heavens and a new earth: in other words, the past will be completely forgotten (Isa. 65:17). The implication of this for Jesus' teaching is that he expects Israel to observe the law, rightly interpreted, until judgement is ended and the people are restored – that is, until all things are accomplished, until God re-establishes his reign over his people and restores the state of creational blessing.

Jesus teaches his disciples to pray that the reign of God will become a reality on earth (Matt. 6:10; cf. 6:33), and we must surely assume that he expected the prayer to be fulfilled. The Lord's Prayer has become for us a sacred object, a resilient sign of the oneness of the church throughout the ages, its sacramental effect heightened by the opacity of its language and thought. Resituated in its narrative context, however, it takes on a distinctive eschatological coloring as a prayer for the coming reign of God. It is a prayer that God's name will no longer be profaned among the nations because of the wretched state of Israel but will be hallowed and vindicated because he has restored his people (cf. Ezek. 36:22–25). It is a prayer that Israel will be delivered from its enemies and that God will reign in place of the present corrupt Jerusalem hierarchy and its Gentile overlords; that the disciples will have their basic material needs met in a time of adversity; that they will share in God's forgiveness of Israel as they forgive those who oppose them; that they will not have to face the testing of persecution; that they will be delivered from the evil power that lurks so menacingly behind Roman imperialism.

The coming of the kingdom will have a direct impact on specific groups in contemporary Israel: the 'poor' and those who are 'persecuted for righteousness' sake' (Matt. 5:3, 10); those among Jesus' hearers who become like little children (Matt. 18:2–4; cf. 19:14; Luke 18:16–17); the wealthy, who will struggle to get through the narrow entrance (Matt. 19:23–24; Mark 10:23–25; Luke 18:24–25); the tax collectors and prostitutes who will go in before the chief priests and elders of the people (Matt. 21:31). The kingdom of God will be taken away from the tenants who rebel against the owner of the vineyard and kill his son and will be given instead to a 'people producing its fruits' (Matt. 21:43); it will be given to Jesus' 'little flock' (Luke 12:32).

Some of Jesus' disciples will be alive to see the 'Son of Man coming in his kingdom' (Matt. 16:28) and the 'kingdom of God after it has come with power' (Mark 9:1; cf. Luke 9:27). The crowds which accompany Jesus into Jerusalem certainly imagine that the coming of the 'kingdom of our father David' is an imminent event (Mark 11:10; cf. Luke 19:38). Just prior to this, Jesus told a parable expressly to correct the impression that the 'kingdom of God was to appear immediately' (Luke 19:11). A nobleman goes into a far country to receive a kingdom. Before he leaves home, he gives a pound to each of ten servants and instructs them to trade with it until he returns. There is a subplot to the parable in Luke that is not found in Matthew's version and which is generally overlooked: the nobleman's subjects send a delegation after him to protest that they do not want him to rule over them; when he eventually returns as king, he calls for his enemies to be brought before him and killed.

Who are these enemies? They must be the defiant, self-serving tenants who murdered the son of the vineyard owner. They are the Jewish authorities who plot to have Jesus arrested and executed. Although the parable introduces a delay before the fulfillment of the kingdom, the nobleman returns soon enough to deal with the rebellious citizens who opposed him. This would be the war against Rome.

The kingdom had already come?

What about the common argument that the kingdom of God is both present and future in Jesus' teaching, that it is both 'now and not yet' – and indeed that the church is still caught in that tension?

When Jesus announces that the kingdom of God is at hand, he has in mind a future event or tide change in the affairs of Israel that will take place within a realistic horizon of relevance for his audience. It will not happen immediately – there will be a period of waiting – but there will be a build-up to it. The call to repentance issued first by John, then by Jesus, and later, of course, by the disciples, results in a limited transformation of Israel that should be regarded as the *present* impact of the announcement about the *future* reign of God. In response to Jesus' preaching, people leave behind their old lives and follow him *for the sake of the future reign of God*. The parables of sowing and growth have this period of waiting in view (Matt. 13:3–9, 18–43; Mark 4:2–20, 26–32; Luke 8:4–15; 13:18–19): the prophetic word of the coming kingdom is sown by Jesus and his disciples; it grows slowly, weeds infest the field, there are various obstacles to fruitfulness, and the effect is negligible at first; but eventually the harvest will come, the crop will bear fruit, the tree will reach maturity, God will act in history to judge his people and establish his righteousness.

Jesus casts out demons in the present *as a prophetic sign* that Satan's control over Israel will not last much longer: the structures of spiritual-political oppression are still in place but that will change (Matt. 12:25–28). He heals the sick *as a prophetic sign* of Israel's coming forgiveness and restoration. The point is that the movement of repentance, forgiveness, restoration, and liberation from oppression which Jesus has started in Israel will reach a climax in a *future* coming of the reign of God. Whatever exactly he means by his retort to the Pharisees that the kingdom of God is 'within you' or 'in the midst of you' (Luke 17:21), he is certainly not saying that the kingdom has already come. His response has to do not with the timing of the coming but with how it will be recognized – not with 'signs to be observed' such that people will be able to say, ' "Look, here it is!" or "There!" ' He goes on to speak of the 'seeing' of the Son of Man in the same terms: 'they will say to you, "Look, there!" or "Look, here!" Do not go out or follow them' (17:23).

There is no great need, therefore, for a mystical 'now-and-not-yet' theory of the kingdom of God. It is conceived in the Gospels as a realistic future event; but the expectation of that event – and the hope that it generates – has an immediate impact on Israel. Let me suggest an analogy. On July 6, 2005, the announcement was made in Singapore that London would host the 2012 Olympic Games. That announcement triggered celebrations, debates, planning, building, hopes, dreams, and not a few anxieties – all in anticipation of a future event. All sorts of sporting events – trials, for example – will be held in the build-up to the Games. These are not the Games, but they anticipate the Games, they gain their significance from a future event that will not be postponed indefinitely but will take place within the foreseeable future of those to whom the announcement is made. The 'good news' that is proclaimed in the Gospels is a message *to Israel and about Israel*. It is essentially an announcement about an event in the foreseeable future that will mean not only judgement and forgiveness for the nation but also defeat of its enemies. This is YHWH coming as king in order to transform the corporate condition of his people. Jesus is not only a prophet – as John is – making this announcement; he is also understood to be the one who will save his people from the historical consequences of their rebelliousness. How? By anticipating in his own *almost theatrical* career the experience of the 'servant' community, which is the servant Jacob, through which the future of the people of the promise will be safeguarded. This salvation will have an impact on the nations, who will acknowledge the righteousness and power of YHWH, but at the moment this is a peripheral consideration.

We will explore these themes further in the coming chapters: first, an image of two roads, one leading to judgement, the other to life; secondly, Jesus' identification with suffering Israel, particularly as the experience is interpreted by the story of the Son of Man; and thirdly, the continuation of that story in the community which he forms around himself. But I would repeat the crucial point for our understanding of mission. This story about the 'salvation' of Israel cannot be regarded as merely the historical husk encasing a gospel of personal salvation and eternal life. The salvation of Israel from its enemies *is* the gospel that is announced. There is nothing else inside it. We need to find some way to connect with this argument, but it will not be by snatching the word 'gospel' – as we might snatch the plate of tarts from the Queen of Hearts – and fleeing with it from this historical Wonderland. It is Jesus' 'gospel,' not ours; we must ask if we can borrow it.

4

The Easy Road Leading to Destruction

'Do not think that I have come to bring peace upon the land. I have not come to bring peace, but a sword' (Matt. 10:34, my translation). I have translated the Greek phrase *epi tēn gēn* here as 'upon the land' rather than 'to the earth' (ESV), with ample precedent in the Septuagint, not least with reference to judgement against a nation (Jer. 25:9, 13; 27:18; 42:11; 44:19 LXX; Ezek. 14:15, 17, 19; 21:7; 25:3, 6; 33:3; 36:6; 38:16, 18).

Jesus, as so often, speaks with the voice of the prophets. Jeremiah, for example, describes the devastation of Judah by Nebuchadnezzar, king of Babylon: 'Upon all the bare heights in the desert destroyers have come, for the sword of the LORD devours from one end of the land to the other; no flesh has peace' (Jer. 12:12). The false prophets who claim that Israel will be spared the sword and famine, that God will 'give you assured peace in this place,' will themselves be consumed by sword and famine along with the people to whom they prophesy – 'them, their wives, their sons, and their daughters' (Jer. 14:13–16). Ezekiel is the 'Son of Man' who is instructed to prophesy against Jerusalem and the land of Israel: 'Behold, I am against you and will draw my sword from its sheath and will cut off from you both righteous and wicked' (Ezek. 21:3). He is the lookout who must warn the people when he sees God bringing a sword upon the land (33:2).

This is not figurative language. The sword that the prophets saw drawn against Israel was a ferocious Babylonian weapon, no less destructive than famine or disease. Jesus' statement is just as realistic. Those who promise peace at a time like this are fools: there will be no peace, only war – a state of upheaval and confusion that will divide households. Under these extreme circumstances only those who are willing to renounce all other loyalties – including even the ties of family – will find life (Matt. 10:37–38).

The dilemma is captured in the image of two divergent roads: through a broad gate is an easy road leading to destruction; through a narrow gate is a difficult and painful road leading to life (Matt. 7:13–14; Luke 13:24). The image is again secondhand, adapted from Jeremiah. Nebuchadnezzar is making war against Jerusalem. King Zedekiah sends a messenger to Jeremiah, hoping to hear from him that YHWH will intervene on behalf of Jerusalem and send Nebuchadnezzar packing. The word of the Lord that comes back from Jeremiah is brutal: 'I myself will fight against you with outstretched hand and strong arm, in anger and in fury and in great wrath' (Jer. 21:5). They will be powerless to defend themselves; if they do not die from disease and starvation, they will be slaughtered by the Babylonian soldiers. The situation, however, is not entirely hopeless. They are given a stark choice: 'Behold, I set before you the way of life and the way of death' (21:8). Those who stay in Jerusalem will die, one way or another; those who leave the city and surrender to the besieging army will live – they will have their lives 'as a prize of war' (21:9).

Jesus makes use of this image of the two roads not to express a universal spiritual choice but because he believes that history is repeating itself. The meaning of the image is controlled by the narrative. If as a nation the Jews refuse to abandon the broad path that they are on, they cannot expect YHWH to avert military disaster – far from it. He himself will fight against them, and many will die from disease, famine, and the sword – which is exactly what we find in the account of the siege of Jerusalem that has come down to us from the Jewish historian Josephus:

So all hope of escaping was now cut off from the Jews, together
with their liberty of going out of the city. Then did the famine
widen its progress, and devoured the people by whole houses
and families; the upper rooms were full of women and children
that were dying by famine; and the lanes of the city were full of
the dead bodies of the aged; the children also and the young men
wandered about the market places like shadows, all swelled with
the famine, and fell down dead wherever their misery seized
them. As for burying them, those who were sick themselves were
not able to do it; and those who were hearty and well were
deterred from doing it by the great multitude of those dead
bodies, and by the uncertainty there was how soon they should
die themselves; for many died as they were burying others, and
many went to their coffins before that fatal hour was come! (*J.W.*
5.12.3 §512–14)

There is, however, an alternative to this horrifying fate – a
narrow gate and a difficult path that begins with repentance,
passes by way of rejection and suffering, and eventually leads
to life.

Another well-known image, no less powerful in its visual
simplicity and no less subject to misapplication, makes the same
point: a house built on a rock will survive the storm-floods; a
house built on the sand will be washed away (Matt. 7:24–27; cf.
Luke 6:47–49). This whole section of Jesus' teaching is strongly
reminiscent of Ezekiel 13:8–16. God denounces the lying
prophets who mislead the people with false hopes of peace for
Jerusalem. The people build a wall, and the prophets daub it
with whitewash, but God will destroy it: 'I will make a stormy
wind break out in my wrath, and there shall be a deluge of rain
in my anger, and great hailstones in wrath to make a full end'
(Ezek. 13:13). Similarly, Jesus warns against 'false prophets, who
come to you in sheep's clothing but inwardly are ravenous
wolves' and those who say 'Lord, Lord,' but do not do the will
of God (Matt. 7:15, 21–23); and he describes the destruction by
storms of the house that the people build. It is perhaps less
certain that Jesus had this actual passage in mind, but the
narrative argument is the same. If Israel builds its house on
delusions, false prophecies, and misplaced hopes, the house

will be destroyed when the judgement of war comes: 'Its end shall come with a flood, and to the end there shall be war' (Dan. 9:26). If Israel builds its house on Jesus' words, then that house will still be standing after the eschatological crisis.

Talking in riddles

The failure of Israel to hear Jesus' words is powerfully and ironically demonstrated by the fact that he spoke to the people in parables. Mystified by the story Jesus told about a sower, the disciples ask him why he teaches in such a riddling fashion. He explains that there are some in Israel who understand the 'secrets of the kingdom of heaven' and others who do not (Matt. 13:11; cf. Mark 4:11; Luke 8:10; cf. also Dan. 11:32). He then quotes the words that Isaiah heard when he was sent by God to speak to Israel: 'Go, and say to this people: "Keep on hearing, but do not understand; keep on seeing, but do not perceive." Make the heart of this people dull, and their ears heavy, and blind their eyes; lest they see with their eyes, and hear with their ears, and understand with their hearts, and turn and be healed' (Isa. 6:9–10). The quotation brings its context with it. In consternation Isaiah asks how long this state of affairs will last, and God answers: 'Until cities lie waste without inhabitant, and houses without people, and the land is a desolate waste, and the LORD removes people far away, and the forsaken places are many in the midst of the land' (6:11–12). Jesus makes use of the whole argument, if only implicitly at this point: if Israel now is unable to grasp the significance of these stories about the reign of God, the consequence will be the devastation of its cities and the scattering of its people.

The simple fact, therefore, that Jesus chooses to communicate the truth about the kingdom of God in parables is itself a sign that destruction is imminent. The same point is made in Matthew 13:34–35 with reference to Psalm 78:2: 'I will open my mouth in a parable; I will utter dark sayings from of old.' What the psalmist recounts is a grim narrative of rebellion, ingratitude, disbelief, and idolatry that culminates in God's utter rejection of the northern kingdom and the sanctuary at

Shiloh. Not mentioned in the Gospels but no less significant is the fact that Ezekiel is instructed to tell parables to the rebellious house of Israel – enigmatic stories about the exile of the people and the siege of Jerusalem (Ezek. 17:2–10; 24:2–14; cf. 20:49). The parables are not fables; they are not vehicles of universal spiritual or moral truth. They are, in both form and content, a warning to stubborn Israel that a tsunami that has been traveling across the ocean of history since the deep spiritual earthquake of the exile is rapidly approaching the shore, bringing destruction and death.

The parable of the sower by its puzzling nature raises the question of why so many in Israel failed to understand the 'word of the kingdom' (Matt. 13:19). But it also provides an answer. The machinations of the evil one, the fear of per-secution, the strain of living under Roman occupation (the 'anxieties of the age'), and the 'deceitfulness of riches' prevent the seed of the word from taking root and flourishing. Only a few really get the point – but they will grow and produce grain in abundance.

The gehenna of fire

The theme of judgement runs right through the Gospel narratives, and at every point along the way we should sense the threat of approaching war, we should see in the mind's eye the distant plume of smoke rising from a city in flames, we should hear the sounds of anger and anguish carried on the wind. The difficulty we face as modern readers, however, is that this historical setting has faded from view, like the body of Lewis Carroll's Cheshire cat, leaving only a lingering apocalyptic smile. In the absence of the rest of the animal, tradition has unwittingly reinterpreted the language and imagery of judgement against a universalized and for the most part metaphysical background. This needs to be undone, start-ing with the traditional notion of 'hell.'

Anyone who is angry with his brother or insults him will be liable to the 'gehenna of fire' (cf. Matt. 5:22). It would be better for a person to cut off his foot or hand or tear out his eye than for his whole body to be thrown into gehenna, into the fire of the age (Mark 9:43–48; cf. Matt. 5:29–30; 18:8–9). Every tree that fails to bear good fruit will be cut down and thrown into the fire (Matt. 7:19). Those branches of the vine of Israel which do not bear fruit, which wither because they have no life, are 'gathered, thrown into the fire, and burned' (John 15:6). The Pharisees cannot expect to escape from the judgement of gehenna – the image is of snakes fleeing for their lives from a burning field (Matt. 23:33; cf. 3:7).

These images of destruction in the 'gehenna of fire' – the 'hell of fire,' as the phrase is often translated – have their origin in Jeremiah's description of the terrible effects of the Babylonian invasion. Because the sons of Judah did what was evil in the sight of the Lord, because they committed idolatry by setting 'their detestable things in the house that is called by my name, to defile it,' because they burned their children as offerings to Molech in the Valley of the Son of Hinnom, God would bring destruction upon them. The Valley of Hinnom would be renamed the Valley of Slaughter into which Jerusalem's dead would be thrown, to be consumed by birds and wild beasts (Jer. 7:30–34).

By Jesus' time the valley of Hinnom, in Greek *geenna*, situated just outside the walls of the city, had become a place of fire, a slow-burning refuse dump. So the judgement of gehenna is now a destruction by fire. When war comes, Jerusalem's dead will again pile up outside the walls of the city – those who die of famine and disease, those crucified by the Romans, those who fall victim to fighting among the insurgents. Josephus describes how the Jewish partisans, for whom he has nothing but contempt, first ordered the dead to be buried at public expense, then when that proved impossible, had them thrown from the walls into the valleys (*J.W.* 5.12.3 §518). This was Jesus' 'hell' – and it could have been avoided.

Mark adds to the image an allusion to the worm and fire of Isaiah 66:24. Following judgement on idolatrous and disobedient Israel, the nations will bring back the scattered Jews to Jerusalem as an offering to the Lord. They will go out from the city and look upon the 'dead bodies of the men who have rebelled against me. For their worm shall not die, their fire shall not be quenched, and they shall be an abhorrence to all flesh.' This is an image of death, the destruction of war, the finality of divine judgement, not of unending torment in hell as the traditional Christian myth has it: the worm may not die, the fire may not be quenched, but corpses do not experience pain. It serves quite simply as a perpetual reminder that the wages of sin, which is in the first place national defiance of the living God, is death (cf. John 8:24), and death can be an appalling, sickening thing. Josephus again brings home the historical reality in his description of the bodies of the insurgents washed up on the shore of Lake Gennesareth following a sea-borne engagement with the Romans: 'as for the shores, they were full of shipwrecks, and of dead bodies all swelled; and as the dead bodies were inflamed by the sun, and putrefied, they corrupted the air, insomuch that the misery was not only the object of pity to the Jews, but to those who hated them and had been the authors of that misery' (*J.W.* 3.10.9 §530). This was the reality of God's wrath against Israel – and it could have been avoided.

The weeds in the field

The kingdom is like a man who sows good seed in his field. When his enemy spoils the crop by sowing weeds, the farmer decides to wait until the harvest before separating out the weeds and burning them (Matt. 13:24–30). Jesus explains the parable. It is a story about the 'Son of man,' who sows the good seed, which represents the 'sons of the kingdom' (RSV). The weeds, sown by the devil, are the 'sons of the evil one.' At the end of the age, the Son of Man will send his angels to gather up everything that is evil and throw it into the fiery furnace. 'Then the righteous will shine like the sun in the kingdom of their Father' (Matt. 13:43).

This last statement in particular alerts us to the fact that the interpretation has been painted over another story – one which is not difficult to discern if we view it in the right light. The Son of Man who sows the good seed is – at least typologically – the 'one like a son of man' who appears in Daniel's vision coming on the clouds of heaven (Dan. 7:13). The 'sons of the kingdom' are the 'saints of the Most High,' who 'shall receive the kingdom and possess the kingdom for ever' (7:18; cf. 14, 22, 27). The 'sons of the evil one' correspond to the disloyal in Israel who are seduced by Antiochus Epiphanes and 'violate the covenant' (11:32). In the aftermath of the great affliction at the close of the age, the wicked will be raised from the dust of the earth to 'shame and everlasting contempt,' but 'those who are wise shall shine like the brightness of the sky above; and those who turn many to righteousness, like the stars for ever and ever' (12:2–3).

In his explanation of the parable Jesus evokes this older vision of Israel facing political-religious crisis and applies it to the situation that the nation faced in the time of Tiberius Caesar, when Pontius Pilate was governor in Judea. The parable describes what the disciples would have to deal with; it addresses their questions about the hostility and duplicity that they would encounter; it provides a rationale for their suffering: the evil one has seduced many in Israel, they have forsaken the covenant, and have become enemies of the righteous. But at the end of the age rebellious Israel will be destroyed; the kingdom will be given to the community represented by the Son of Man; and the 'righteous will shine like the sun in the kingdom of their Father' (Matt. 13:43).

The parable of the net has the same frame of reference (Matt. 13:47–50). At the close of the age a net will be thrown into the sea, the good fish will be sorted from the bad, the righteous from the unrighteous. It concludes with the same disturbing refrain: 'In that place there will be weeping and gnashing of teeth' – the weeping of Jews suffering judgement and the gnashing of teeth of their enemies. This is not some lurid metaphysical hell that Jesus describes: it is the horror of war. Rebellious Israel will be destroyed; the righteous will be preserved, one way or another.

The day of judgement

Jesus speaks repeatedly of a day of judgement when the nation will be held to account for its failure to hear the prophetic voice and pursue the things that make for peace – literal peace, peace rather than war (cf. Luke 19:42). Towns and villages that reject the disciples when they are sent out to proclaim the imminence of the kingdom of God will suffer more than the land of Sodom and Gomorrah on the 'day of judgement' (Matt. 10:15). Cities such as Chorazin and Bethsaida that did not repent when they saw the 'mighty works' that Jesus performed will fare worse than Tyre and Sidon on the 'day of judgement.' Capernaum will be 'brought down to Hades' – destroyed in the war, its inhabitants killed. The people of Nineveh will rise up at the judgement and condemn this generation of Israel because of their refusal to repent (Matt. 12:41; Luke 11:32). If the Jews do not repent, they will be killed – just as the Galileans were killed by Pilate as they offered sacrifice, just as eighteen people died in Siloam when a tower collapsed on them (Luke 13:1–5).

People will 'give account for every careless word they speak' on the 'day of judgement' (Matt. 12:36). When Jesus hears that the Pharisees were offended by a remark about people being defiled by what comes out of the mouth, his response is that 'Every plant that my heavenly Father has not planted will be rooted up' (Matt. 15:13). The cursing of the fig tree on the way to Jerusalem is a sign that Israel has failed to bear fruit and will be condemned: it is the barren fig tree of the parable that will be cut down, if not this year then next (Matt. 21:19; Mark 11:13–14; Luke 13:6–9). The master of the house, whose servants first and then son are killed by the malcontent tenants of his vineyard, will put them to a miserable death and let out the vineyard to other tenants (Matt. 21:41; Mark 12:9; Luke 20:16). When those invited to the wedding feast of the king's son refuse to attend and, worse, abuse and murder his servants, the king will send his troops to destroy them and burn their city (Matt. 22:7). Judgement will come on 'this generation' because they have shed the blood of the righteous prophets (Matt. 23:34–36; Luke 11:50–51). Israel's house – a reference to the temple – will be 'left to you desolate' because they killed the prophets and rejected the path of salvation (Matt. 23:37–38; Luke 13:34–35).

Ground zero on the day of judgement will be the temple. The first thing Jesus does on arriving in Jerusalem is to enter the vast court of the nations and drive out all those who sold and bought there. In explanation of this disruptive action he links together two Old Testament texts. The first is Isaiah's prophecy of a time when foreigners will join themselves to the Lord and bring their sacrifices to the altar, when the temple will be known as 'a house of prayer for all peoples' (Isa. 56:6–7). But this salvation will come about *only if* they 'keep justice, and do righteousness' (56:1). They do not. The second text is Jeremiah's scathing attack on a people who 'steal, murder, commit adultery, swear falsely, make offerings to Baal, and go after other gods that you have not known' and then have the effrontery to stand before YHWH in the temple and say, 'We are delivered!' In effect, they have made the temple a 'den of robbers,' a refuge for a corrupt and unjust hierarchy, a sanctuary for a rebellious people (Jer. 7:11). So God will destroy the temple just as he destroyed the sanctuary at Shiloh (7:12–15).

The prospect of war

Jesus tells the disciples what to expect as the day approaches when the buildings of the temple will be demolished and the city devastated (Matt. 23:38; 24:1–3), when Jerusalem will be surrounded by its enemies, torn down to the ground, and its inhabitants killed (Luke 19:43–44; cf. 21:20). False Christs and false prophets will lead many in Judea astray. They will hear rumors of impending war; nations will come into conflict; there will be famines and earthquakes. These are only the beginning of the 'birth pains.' The disciples will face severe opposition; some of them will be killed. The temple will be desecrated by an unclean pagan presence in the holy place – an abomination that makes desolate. Great distress will come upon the land, wrath upon this people; they will 'fall by the edge of the sword and be led captive among all nations, and Jerusalem will be trampled underfoot by the Gentiles' – a 'great tribulation, such as has not been from the beginning of the world until now, no, and never will be' (Matt. 24:4–28; Mark 13:4–23; Luke 21:6–24).

   None of this belongs to the end of history. Jesus sketches a historical scenario that the disciples would have found entirely realistic. The easiest way to demonstrate this is to draw attention to Josephus' scornful account of the confusion and suffering caused by numerous false prophets and royal pretenders during the war against Rome – the 'Egyptian false prophet,' for example, who led thousands to their deaths in an attempt to seize Jerusalem from the Romans, or the 'cheats and deceivers' who claimed divine inspiration and 'schemed to bring about revolutionary changes by inducing the mob to act as if possessed, and by leading them out into the wild country on the pretence that there God would show them signs of approaching freedom' (J.W. 2.13.4–5 §258–64; cf. Acts 21:38). He also records extraordinary phenomena that presaged the desolation of the temple: a star resembling a sword above the city, a comet that lasted for a year, a bright light that appeared around the altar of the temple, a heifer that gave birth to a lamb as it was led to be sacrificed, the opening of the eastern temple gate of its own accord, a vision of chariots and soldiers in the clouds at sunset surrounding the cities of Judah, the sound of quaking and a great noise in the sanctuary and the voices of a multitude saying, 'We are departing from here' (J.W. 6.5.3 §288–300). We do not have to believe that all these things actually happened, but the account helps us to understand how easily Jesus' apocalypticism would have been interpreted with reference to the fall of Jerusalem.

Jesus also means the disciples to hear echoes of earlier accounts of divine judgement. For example, this is how Jeremiah warns of Nebuchadnezzar's invasion to put down Zedekiah's foolish rebellion: 'behold, there comes a rumor of a noise and a great earthquake from a northern country, to appoint the cities of Judah for destruction' (Jer. 10:22 LXX, my translation). The phrase 'abomination of desolation' originally referred to the imposition of a Syrian garrison in the fortress and temple area of Jerusalem, with their worship of the god Baal Samem (Dan. 11:31). Daniel also describes the climactic judgement of Jerusalem as a 'time of trouble, such as never has been since there was a nation till that time' (Dan. 12:1); and indeed Josephus wrote of the war in similar terms: 'the misfortunes of all men from the beginning of the world, if they be compared to these of the Jews are not so considerable as they were'; 'the multitude of those that therein perished exceeded all the destructions that either men or God ever brought upon the world' (*J.W.* Proem 4 §12; 6.9.4).

All this would come about within a generation: the persecution of the disciples, the chaotic build-up to war, the destruction of the city by the Gentiles. Just as the appearance of leaves on a tree is a sign that summer is near, so these events will be a sign to the inhabitants of Jerusalem that the kingdom is given to the Son of Man and to the disciples, who have chosen the other road, that their vindication is near (Luke 21:27–33).

Judgement means destruction and death for Israel – not metaphorical or spiritual death, but real death, the sort of unnatural and horrifying death that comes with insurrection, war, starvation, and disease. Salvation in the Gospels, therefore, must mean survival and life – in equally realistic and historical terms. When the storm comes, as it inevitably will, everything that has been built on the sand will collapse and be washed away; only the community that has been built on the rock of Jesus' teaching will still be standing when the floods subside. So as we reconstruct the narrative of mission that emerges from the Gospels, we must ask how the hope of 'salvation' is conceived. What does Jesus have in mind when he speaks of an alternative road leading to *life*?

5

The Difficult Road Leading to Life

The preaching of the kingdom of God in the Gospels is from the start inseparable from the activity of healing. Matthew's succinct account is characteristic: 'he went throughout all Galilee, teaching in their synagogues and proclaiming the gospel of the kingdom and healing every disease and every affliction among the people' (Matt. 4:23; cf. 9:35). Unsurprisingly this attracted the crowds: 'they brought him all the sick, those afflicted with various diseases and pains, those oppressed by demons, epileptics, and paralytics, and he healed them.' People were, of course, astonished by these remarkable occurrences, but their significance lies not so much in their capacity to elicit wonder or even worship as in their storytelling potential. They are parabolic, narrative events. They form part of Jesus' telling and retelling of the story of Israel.

This observation can be investigated along three lines. First, the healings are a sign of forgiveness and of the reversal of judgement. Secondly, the expulsion of demons signals the defeat of the spiritual power that wields the forces of oppression against the people of God. Thirdly, by his compassion for the afflicted Jesus shows himself to be the good shepherd of a restored Israel.

Restoration and forgiveness

The healings are to be seen, in the first place, as concrete signs of the forgiveness of Israel and the restoration of the creational microcosm. Deuteronomy 28:15–68 presents a lengthy catalogue of the disasters that will come upon the people of Israel if they fail to obey the voice of God and keep the commandments and statutes given by Moses (Deut. 28:15). Essentially these curses constitute a failure or reversal of the well-being and prosperity associated with the land – in other words, a failure of the localized reinstatement of creation that was promised through Abraham. The fecundity of the land will be ruined by blight and drought; enemies will invade and plunder its produce; and the people will go into captivity and exile – they will be *dislocated* from the land. The creational blessing has broken down. But it is the curse of sickness that we need especially to note. The people will suffer extreme afflictions and sicknesses until they are destroyed – no longer 'as numerous as the stars of heaven,' no longer being multiplied in number as a new humanity, but reduced to a pitiful few (28:58–63). For Jesus to heal large numbers of people as an expression of the 'gospel of the kingdom' must be understood in light of this. It is a sign that the damage done to the creational microcosm is being repaired, that the period of judgement is coming to an end, that a new life is emerging.

Matthew sees in the healing of the sick a fulfillment of Isaiah's statement: 'He took our illnesses and bore our diseases' (Matt. 8:17). The servant of the Lord described in this passage is one who exhibits in his person the consequences of Israel's sin. He was wounded because of Israel's transgressions, bruised because of Israel's iniquities (Isa. 53:5). The language recalls Deuteronomy 28:59–61. He is acquainted with 'sickness'; he has borne our 'sicknesses' (Isa. 53:3–4), which is the sickness that would be inflicted upon the people of Israel if they do not keep the commandments (Deut. 28:59, 61). God has 'smitten' or 'struck' him (53:4) just as the Lord would strike disobedient Israel with 'wasting disease and with fever, inflammation and fiery heat,' with the 'boils of Egypt, and with tumours and scabs and itch,' and with 'madness and blindness and confusion of mind' (Deut. 28:22, 27, 28; cf. 35). The servant suffers in his body, taking upon himself the physical or creational effects of the curse on Israel. His disfigured appearance and the contempt in which he is held by men (Isa. 52:14; 53:3) correspond to Israel's wretched and diminished status in the world: 'you shall become a horror, a proverb, and a byword among all the peoples where the LORD will lead you away' (Deut. 28:37). The servant is deformed because sinful Israel is deformed, sick because sinful Israel is sick.

So Matthew's simple allusion to Isaiah's account of the servant who carries Israel's illnesses and diseases stands as far more than a proof of Jesus' identity. It is an *interpretation* of his healing actions within a narrative of judgement and restoration that carries – we should not lose sight of this – persistent creational overtones. This reading does not require us to think that sickness in Israel, or any particular instance of sickness in Israel, was a direct consequence of Israel's sin. Jesus carefully avoids that inference – quite explicitly in John 9:2–3, when the disciples ask whether a man's blindness should be attributed to his own or his parents' sin. Jesus denies the connection with personal sinfulness, but the man's condition provides an opportunity to demonstrate what God is doing. The point is that by healing the sick Jesus is acting out – both as a prophetic parable and as the premature impact of the kingdom of God – the restoration of a people suffering from the judgement described in Deuteronomy 28. Healing is a sign of forgiveness.

The announcement of forgiveness must be heard against the background buzz of passages such as Daniel's prayer of confession on behalf of the people. Israel has acted wickedly and rebelled and, therefore, justly suffers extreme punishment – 'under the whole heaven there has not been done anything like what has been done against Jerusalem' (Dan. 9:12). Daniel brings the supplications of the exiled people to God not 'because of our righteousness, but because of your great mercy' and seeks forgiveness and an end to the wrath of God against Jerusalem (9:18–19). Similarly, Zechariah's statement concerning John that he would 'go before the Lord to prepare his ways, to give knowledge of salvation to his people in the forgiveness of their sins' (Luke 1:76–77) recalls the assurance to Jerusalem in

Isaiah 40:2 'that her warfare is ended, that her iniquity is pardoned, that she has received from the LORD's hand double for all her sins.'

When the Pharisees raise questions about Jesus' habit of eating with 'tax collectors and sinners,' he tells them that it is not the healthy but the sick who need a physician; then he advises them to go and look up Hosea 6:6: 'I desire mercy, and not sacrifice' (Matt. 9:13). The people of Israel will take their sacrificial animals to the temple, but they will not find the Lord there (Hos. 5:6). He has withdrawn from them until they acknowledge their guilt and seek his face, saying: 'Come, let us return to the LORD; for he has torn us, that he may heal us; he has struck us down, and he will bind us up. After two days he will revive us; on the third day he will raise us up, that we may live before him' (Hos. 6:1–2). Here is the point of the saying about the physician. Israel is figuratively sick because it is under judgement; if the people repent and turn to the Lord, they will be healed – and significantly (we will come back to this) will be raised up on the third day to live before God. The tax collectors and sinners then represent that part of the population that turns to the Lord in its distress looking for healing and resurrection.

This background narrative also helps to explain the connection between healing and forgiveness. There is a well-known incident that took place in Capernaum when a paralyzed man was lowered through the roof of the house because there was no other way to reach Jesus (Matt. 9:2–8; Mark 2:1–12; Luke 5:17–26). Jesus' immediate response to this faithful act of vandalism was not to heal but to pronounce the forgiveness of the man's sins. Knowing that the Pharisees and scribes present were offended by this, he asks them, 'Which is easier, to say to the paralytic, "Your sins are forgiven", or to say, "Rise, take up your bed and walk"?' (Mark 2:9). He then heals the man, and everyone is astonished; but the important point to note is that he connects this with Daniel's story about the Son of Man: the healing is a sign that 'the Son of Man has authority on earth to forgive sins' (2:10).

This narrative is evoked by Jesus' response to the scribes and Pharisees crowded into the house: the Son of Man has received authority on earth from the Ancient of Days, among other things to pronounce the forgiveness of Israel's sins and to demonstrate the effectiveness of that pronouncement through an act of healing. What makes this controversial is not that Jesus claims to be God. When the scribes accuse him of blasphemy, they are not saying that he imagines himself to be God. Their point is that he does not have the *authority* to forgive sins, because God has reserved that right for himself (cf. Isa. 43:25; 44:22; Jer. 31:34; 33:8; 36:3; Ezek. 16:63; Mic. 7:19). Jesus' argument is that this right *has been given to the Son of Man*, to the one who represents suffering, faithful Israel; and, indeed, that the whole apocalyptic narrative of judgement, forgiveness and the vindication of the faithful, is being fulfilled. The response of the crowds is not to acclaim Jesus as God but to glorify the God who has given this authority *to men* (Matt. 9:8).

The defeat of the enemy

In the Old Testament, Satan is the 'accuser' or 'prosecutor' of Israel in the heavenly court: he incites David to number Israel (1 Chr. 21:1); he tests Job's righteousness by subjecting him to severe suffering (Job 1 – 2); and he is seen by Zechariah in a vision standing at the right hand of Joshua the high priest to accuse him (Zech. 3:1–2). The encounter with Satan in the Gospels is bound up with Israel's experience of being accused or opposed at a time of eschatological crisis. Satan is not present as an abstract metaphysical or occult entity. He is present as a challenge to Israel as it struggles to find the path that leads to life.

Satan endeavors to trip up Jesus, who has chosen to *be* Israel, on his journey of obedience through the wilderness toward the renewal of the people of God. He speaks through Jesus' closest friends in an attempt to divert him from his commitment to endure, as the Son of Man, the suffering that Israel would have to suffer because of its sins. Just as YHWH rebukes the accuser of Joshua in Zechariah 3:2, Jesus defies Satan: 'Be gone, Satan! Get behind me, Satan!' (Matt. 4:10; 16:23). Satan prevents the word of the kingdom of God from taking root in people's hearts (Mark 4:15). He has sought permission from God to sift the disciples (the 'you' in Luke 22:31 is plural) like wheat – to test their commitment and integrity through suffering – but Jesus has prayed that their faith will not fail. The same thought is expressed in the Lord's Prayer: 'lead us not into temptation, but deliver us from the evil one' (Matt. 6:13, my translation). In the background may be the image of sifting as judgement on 'the sinful kingdom' found in Amos 9:8–9: God will 'shake the house of Israel among all the nations as one shakes with a sieve, but no pebble shall fall to the earth.' The faith of the disciples will be severely tested in the coming years, but the implicit assurance is that none of them will fall through the sieve, none will be lost – except the 'son of destruction' (John 17:12).

The experience of being opposed is not merely spiritual or internal: it is people – neighbors, councils, magistrates, rulers – who will accuse and condemn the disciples. Satan inevitably, therefore, comes to be associated with the social, religious, and political bodies that are affronted by the disciples' activity. Eventually the confrontation with Roman imperialism will be re-imagined as the war between the little horn on the head of the fourth beast and the saints of the Most High that is described in Daniel 7:19–27 (cf. 2 Thess. 2:3–12; Rev. 13:1–18).

There are indications, however, that the reign of Satan as Israel's adversary is coming to an end. When the seventy-two return and tell Jesus that 'even the demons are subject to us in your name,' he sees in this a sign of the imminent and decisive defeat of the eschatological opponent: 'I saw Satan fall like lightning from heaven.' The disciples have been given the authority that belongs to the Son of Man to overcome 'all the power of the enemy' (Luke 10:17–19). By casting out demons Jesus demonstrates that Satan's power over Israel has been curbed – the strong man has been bound and his house can be plundered in order to rescue a remnant who will become renewed Israel (Matt. 12:28–29). In Luke's version of the story Jesus casts out demons by the 'finger of God,' recalling the anxious words of the magicians to Pharaoh when they could not replicate the spawning of gnats from the dust of the earth: 'This is the finger of God' (Exod. 8:19; Luke 11:20). This is not accidental. It reinforces the connection between the presence of the demonic and Israel's condition of political oppression. The

overthrowing of the adversary and the coming of the reign of
God encompass the defeat of Rome.

Two other incidents are worth reading in this light. The first
is the healing of the Gerasene demoniac (Mark 5:1–20; Matt.
8:28–34; Luke 8:26–39). The 'unclean spirit' that possessed the
man identifies itself as 'Legion,' which immediately associates it
with a brutal Roman occupying force. The uncleanness of this
disturbing 'military' presence on the borders of Israel is
underlined by the location (the man lives among the tombs) and
the proximity of a herd of pigs.

Secondly, Jesus tells a story about an unclean spirit that leaves
a person, wanders through waterless places, and eventually
returns to its original 'house' with 'seven other spirits more evil
than itself' (Matt. 12:43–45). The important thing to note is that
this parable is directed explicitly at 'this evil generation,' a
generation that faces judgement (12:41–42). It is a parable about
Israel. The increase in demonic activity is linked to the
disintegration of religious and political life that will culminate
in war and the destruction of Jerusalem. The parable is a
warning to the scribes and Pharisees: Jesus may cast out
demons now, but they will be back with a vengeance and will
bring the nation to ruin. Josephus describes the madness with
which the Jews brought destruction upon themselves. Note in
particular the reference to a 'diseased body':

> Now when these were quieted, it happened, as it does in a
> diseased body, that another part was subject to an inflammation;
> a company of deceivers and robbers got together, and persuaded
> the Jews to revolt, and exhorted them to assert their liberty,
> inflicting death on those who continued in obedience to the
> Roman government, and saying, that such as willingly chose
> slavery, ought to be forced from their desired inclinations; for
> they parted themselves into different bodies, and lay in wait up
> and down the country, and plundered the houses of the great
> men, and slew the men themselves, and set the villages on fire;
> and this till all Judea was filled with the effects of their madness.
> And thus the flame was every day more and more blown up, till
> it came to a direct war. (*J.W.*, 2.13.6 §264–65)

The alternative to the ruthless hegemony of Rome is enacted in the carefully staged prophetic event of the entry into Jerusalem. We might hesitate to call it a 'publicity stunt,' but that would not be too far wide of the mark – especially if Borg and Crossan are correct in their view that on the same day, across the city, Pilate would have been entering Jerusalem in a display of imperial presence and military power in order to keep a firm lid on nationalist sentiments during the Passover festival.[1] Whether Jesus had actually arranged matters in advance we have no way of knowing; but in sending two of his disciples to requisition a donkey he makes clear his intention to act out the script of Zechariah's prophecy: 'Rejoice greatly, O daughter of Zion! Shout aloud, O daughter of Jerusalem! behold, your king is coming to you; righteous and having salvation is he, humble and mounted on a donkey, on a colt, the foal of a donkey' (Zech. 9:9).

The verse comes from an oracle against the nations which threaten Israel, and we should assume that by laying implicit claim to be Israel's king in this way, Jesus was also making a statement about the political circumstances that the people of Jerusalem faced. The preceding verse reads: 'Then I will encamp at my house as a guard, so that none shall march to and fro; no oppressor shall again march over them, for now I see with my own eyes' (9:8). The following verse speaks of God cutting off the chariot from Ephraim and the war horse from Jerusalem. Jesus must have been aware that these subversive connotations came trailing noisily behind him like a string of tin cans, as the donkey picked its way up the stony road toward the city gates, passing the wary and bemused Roman soldiers stationed along the route. This humble king brought salvation to an occupied city, and the crowd appears to have understood this much at least. The acclamation 'Blessed is he who comes in the name of the Lord!' (Matt. 21:9; Mark 11:9; Luke 19:38; John 12:13) is from Psalm 118:26, which celebrates the deliverance of Israel's king – and therefore of righteous Israel in him – from those who hate him, from the nations that surround him on every side (7, 10–11). 'Hosanna!' is a Greek transliteration of an Aramaic expression meaning 'O save.' It echoes Psalm 118:25: 'Save us, we pray, O LORD! O LORD, we pray, give us success!' Jesus is welcomed – as Zechariah, the father of John, had foreseen – as the king from the house of David who would save the inhabitants of Jerusalem 'from our enemies, and from the hand of all who hate us' (Luke 1:69–71, cf. 74). This is the hope – a thoroughly political and national hope – that runs through the Gospels.

The good shepherd

The healings are also a sign that Jesus is the true shepherd of Israel. If the nation faces political-religious meltdown, it is not least because the hierarchy in Jerusalem is godless and corrupt. Herod Antipas silenced the prophet John for reasons of political and personal expediency and also sought to kill Jesus (Matt. 14:3–12; Luke 3:19–20; 13:31). The wealthy and powerful, for the most part, treat the poor and helpless with contempt (cf. Luke 16:14–31). The scribes and Pharisees are lambasted as self-serving hypocrites, neglectful of the weightier matters of the law, full of greed and self-indulgence, whitewashed tombs, a brood of vipers (Matt. 23:1–36). Jesus' anger is shocking.

The result of this dereliction of duty is that there are many in Israel who are 'lost.' This language of being 'lost' has itself rather gone astray in our modern missional discourse and needs to be returned to the fold of the biblical narrative – and, we may dare to imagine, great will be the rejoicing in heaven. So when Jesus is overwhelmed by the physical and spiritual needs of the people, Matthew comments that he has compassion on the crowds because they are 'harassed and helpless, like sheep without a shepherd' (Matt. 9:36). The allusion is principally to Ezekiel 34:1–24, where we find a familiar story about Israel. The shepherds of Israel have not cared for the sheep but have exploited them. They have not strengthened the weak, healed the sick, bound up the crippled, or brought back the lost. The sheep have been scattered abroad, they have become prey to wild beasts, harassed and helpless. But God will rescue the sheep from the abusive shepherds; he will bring them back from the places of exile; he will bind up the crippled and strengthen the weak; and he will be their shepherd.

So when Jesus heals the sick and feeds the hungry, he is playing the part of YHWH who takes responsibility for those who are neglected by the corrupt shepherds. When he organizes the disciples to do the same work of preaching the gospel and healing the sick because the 'harvest is plentiful, but the laborers are few' (Matt. 9:37), he is in effect staging a coup d'état. This is not a model for global evangelism. It is an incident in a prophetic and proleptic drama in which Jesus plays – with extraordinary audacity – the part of YHWH who is scripted to reconstitute Israel *from among the lost*. He is the shepherd who goes looking for a lost sheep or the woman who sweeps her house until she finds her lost coin; and God, of course, is the father who celebrates the return of the wayward son (Luke 15:3–32).

From what is lost Jesus creates a community that has experienced both as a fact and as prophetic expectation the forgiveness and freedom from oppression that is to be found down the narrow path that leads to life – because 'it is not the will of my Father who is in heaven that one of these little ones should perish' (Matt. 18:14). Again it must be made clear: this is not the language of a generic, one-size-fits-all salvation; it has to fit the historical narrative. These 'little ones' are those in Israel who are prepared to trust the prophetic voice of Jesus; for them not to 'perish' would be to avoid the devastation of war.

They are a community of the 'have nots,' rescued for the most part from the margins of Israel's social, religious, and political life, invited in from the streets of the city and the surrounding countryside to join in the wedding feast, who will find themselves unexpectedly participating in the renewal of the family of Abraham. It is a community of those who forgive one another because God has offered forgiveness to Israel. It is a community that will embrace those who have been scattered as a result of judgement (cf. Luke 13:29; John 11:49–52). It is a community that shares Jesus' dangerous prophetic function, preaching the same good news of the impending reign of God, casting out demons and healing the sick as a sign that judgement is coming to a climax, that Israel is being restored.

Above all, they form a community that associates itself with Jesus in his suffering. His disciples have left behind their old lives; they have taken up the cross. Whenever they gather together to eat, they will remind themselves through a simple makeshift ritual that they have been brought together to share in the fate of one who gave himself for the future of the people of God. They constitute a community fashioned from the 'poor' of Israel to endure the great tribulation of the end of the age.

A few crumbs for the Gentiles

Did Jesus imagine that Gentiles would be included in this community? Apparently not. The participation of the Gentiles in the salvation of Israel is barely envisaged in the Gospels. John berated the Pharisees and Sadducees who came to him fleeing 'from the wrath to come': the fact that they were physical descendants of Abraham would not save them from destruction; God can raise up children for Abraham from the stones if necessary (Matt. 3:7–9). He may have had the Gentiles in view, but it seems more likely that this is a rhetorical means of underlining the point that the leaders of Israel are not guaranteed political survival.

Jesus does not allow his disciples to preach the good news of the reign of God among the Gentiles or in the towns of the Samaritans; they are to go only to the lost sheep of the house of Israel, who have been neglected and abused by their shepherds (Matt. 10:5–7; cf. Ezek. 34:1–16). The 'other sheep' of John 10:16 may refer to the scattered Jews of the Diaspora rather than to Gentiles (cf. John 11:51–52). It has often been supposed that the parable of the man who gave a great banquet implies a mission to the Gentiles (Luke 14:15–24). When the invited guests refuse to attend, he sends out his servants first into the streets of the city to bring in the 'poor and crippled and blind and lame'; then when there is still room, he sends them out again to compel people to come in from the highways and hedges around the town. But whether Jesus saw in this last group Gentiles who would attach themselves to a renewed Israel is not clear.

At best it is a matter of scavenging for leftovers. The Canaanite woman who is brutally told that she should not expect to eat the bread that is provided for the children of Israel nevertheless gets what she asks for because her faith is great (Matt. 15:22–28). Similarly, Jesus is astonished by the faith of the Roman centurion who believes that he will heal his servant by a word of command, much as he himself would give commands to the men under his authority. Jesus takes it as a sign that 'many will come from east and west and recline at table with Abraham, Isaac, and Jacob in the kingdom of heaven, while the sons of the kingdom will be thrown into the outer darkness' (Matt. 8:11–12). But still, this is a vision of the inclusion of Gentiles *in the restoration of Israel.*

Jesus makes an announcement of 'good news,' not to the whole world but to Israel at a critical juncture in its history, at a fork in the road. There is a broad path which will lead inevitably to destruction. But there is also a narrow path, a way of repentance and forgiveness, that will lead to life. This 'life' is the life of the age to come and must be understood, in the first place, as the continued, transformed existence of the faithful community beyond the eschatological horizon of judgement on Israel. This is Jesus' *gospel.* It is not that he died for my sins. It is not that by believing in him I can please God and go to heaven. It is not that God loves me and has a plan for my life. These things may or may not become relevant later. For now we must hear the announcement within the narrow passageway of the historical narrative. It is that God will bring judgement to a climax within the foreseeable future but will deliver the community that has left the broad path and followed the Son of Man toward life. What we come to next is the question of what it means to walk that narrow path – first for Jesus, then for the community that he gathered around himself from the margins of Jewish life.

6

How Jesus Tells the Story of the Son of Man

Paul reminds the believers in Corinth of the gospel which he preached to them, by which they are being saved: that 'Christ died for our sins in accordance with the Scriptures, that he was buried, that he was raised on the third day in accordance with the Scriptures' (1 Cor. 15:3–4). Usually we would locate this in an argument about personal salvation, along the lines of: Christ died for my sins, God raised him from the dead, if I confess my sins and believe in him, I will have eternal life. If, however, we take the repeated phrase 'in accordance with the Scriptures' seriously, we will have to reposition Jesus' death and resurrection – at least in the first place – in a narrative about Israel that moves from the suffering of the people under judgement through restoration to vindication and kingdom.

The talk about suffering comes as a shock to the disciples, and we are bound to sympathize with them. Peter has arrived at the critical realization that Jesus is the Christ, the Son of the living God, the one who will save Israel from the historical consequences of its sins (Matt. 16:16; cf. Mark 8:29; Luke 9:20). Jesus' response to this, as Matthew's more detailed version has it, is very significant. First, he tells Peter that he is the rock on which he will build his *ekklēsia* – the assembly of Israel gathered before the Lord – and promises him that the 'gates of Hades will not overpower it' (my translation). This last statement has nothing to do with spiritual warfare in the popular sense: we are not to think of hoards of demons rushing out of the gates of hell to attack the church. The phrase 'gates of Hades' is an Old Testament idiom for 'death' (e.g. Isa. 38:10). What Jesus means is that death will not overcome the community that is founded on Peter. Secondly, he says that he will give Peter the 'keys of the kingdom of heaven.' This is a difficult phrase to pin down, but I would argue, particularly in light of what follows, that it brings into view the giving of kingdom and authority to the Son of Man when he comes to the throne of the Ancient of Days (Dan. 7:14, 27). Peter is given the authority or power of the Son of Man who suffered in order to lead an emerging alternative Israel that will not be overcome by death, that will not be persecuted into extinction.

Jesus goes on to tell a concise but coherent story about the Son of Man. He will have to suffer many things: he will be rejected by the leaders of the nation – the elders, chief priests, and scribes – and killed; he will be raised on the third day; and he will come 'in his glory and the glory of the Father and of the holy angels' (Luke 9:26). Boxed within it is a challenge to those who wish to follow him: 'If anyone would come after me, let him deny himself and take up his cross daily and follow me. For whoever would save his life will lose it, but whoever loses his life for my sake will save it' (Mark 8:34–35). The story is told again on the final journey to Jerusalem. When the disciples are fretting about the fact that they have left everything to follow him (Matt. 19:27–30; Luke 18:28–30) and jostling for poll position in the kingdom of God (Matt. 20:20–21), he repeats the prediction: 'See, we are going up to Jerusalem, and everything that is written about the Son of Man by the prophets will be accomplished. For he will be delivered over to the Gentiles and will be mocked and shamefully treated and spat upon. And after flogging him, they will kill him, and on the third day he will rise' (Luke 18:31–33; cf. Matt. 20:18–19).

The telling of this story in connection with Peter's confession, the founding of a community that will not be overcome by death, and the determination to go to Jerusalem, is pivotal in the Gospel narratives. The conclusion is straightforward: Jesus understood his foreseen suffering at the hands of the Gentiles to correspond to the ill-treatment of the Son of Man community by the blasphemous pagan ruler in Daniel 7. This is not simply an appeal to prophecy in order to validate his credentials as the Christ. He must have known that the story was originally conceived with reference to the crisis provoked by Antiochus Epiphanes' aggressive meddling in Jewish religious affairs; but he *re-imagines* it, *retells* it, with a new, analogous, but far more serious calamity in mind. He finds an old cloak in the dressing-up box of Israel's memory, makes some minor adjustments to get it to fit, then wraps himself in it to startling and dramatic effect.

In a deliberate, creative and provocative way he takes upon himself not simply the christological title of 'Son of Man' but the whole story. First, he identifies himself with the suffering community of the righteous in Israel, oppressed by a vicious pagan power: as he says, the Son of Man will suffer and be killed. Secondly, he lays claim to the hope expressed in Daniel 12:2–3 that the righteous who are killed will be raised to 'everlasting life': the Son of Man will be raised from the dead. Thirdly, he predicts the eventual overthrow of the oppressor and the vindication of the Son of Man: he will come in the glory of his Father to repay every man for what he has done. This three-part story needs to be considered in greater detail.

The suffering of Israel

In Daniel's extended narrative of political-religious crisis, the period of wrath against Israel comes to a head when a king of Greece makes war against the people of God and desolates the temple. Many Jews will collaborate with the invader and forsake the covenant. Those 'who know their God shall stand firm and take action,' but they will suffer for their faithfulness: 'the wise among the people shall make many understand, though for some days they shall stumble by sword and flame, by captivity and plunder' (Dan. 11:32–33). These are the saints of the Most High, who in Daniel 7 are symbolized by the figure of the Son of Man: they suffer as the long atonement for iniquity approaches its dénouement, but through their suffering an 'everlasting righteousness' is brought in (Dan. 9:24); in the end, the oppressor is destroyed and the saints are vindicated –

justified, shown to be right for not having colluded with the enemy in the subversion of the covenant.

In the first place, therefore, Jesus identifies himself with the faithful community which suffers at the hands of the Gentiles because the wrath of God against Israel is rapidly approaching a catastrophic endgame. The saying about the Son of Man coming 'not to be served but to serve, and to give his life as a ransom for many' has the same ideological background (Matt. 20:28; Mark 10:45). It is remarkably anticipated in the stories of the Maccabean martyrs, who were subjected to appalling torments and killed by Antiochus because of their loyalty to the traditions of their fathers:

> I, like my brothers, give up body and life for the laws of our fathers, appealing to God to show mercy soon to our nation and by afflictions and plagues to make you confess that he alone is God, and through me and my brothers to bring to an end the wrath of the Almighty which has justly fallen on our whole nation. (2 Macc. 7:37–38 RSV)

> These, then, who have been consecrated for the sake of God, are honored, not only with this honor, but also by the fact that because of them our enemies did not rule over our nation, the tyrant was punished, and the homeland purified – they having become, as it were, a ransom for the sin of our nation. And through the blood of those devout ones and their death as an atoning sacrifice, divine Providence preserved Israel that previously had been mistreated. (4 Macc. 17:20–22 RSV; cf. 4 Macc. 15:24; 16:22; 17:2)

The martyrs whose stories are told here – the elderly scribe Eleazar, the seven brothers and their mother – suffer because of the sin of the nation. Their deaths are understood as the means by which the wrath of God is ended, Israel is liberated from oppression, the enemy of Israel is punished, and the nation is purified and restored. They are, in effect, the 'saints' of Daniel 7:15–27 against whom the little horn makes war and are therefore proper precursors of Jesus' 'Son of Man' who must be rejected by the corrupt leadership in Jerusalem and killed by the Gentiles.

The Son of Man narrative, therefore, is a story about the salvation of the people of Israel from the crisis precipitated by Antiochus Epiphanes' ferocious attack on its religious identity. For the sake of the covenant the righteous suffer, but through their suffering the nation is preserved. If, as seems likely, Jesus also had in mind Isaiah's 'servant,' who 'poured out his soul to death . . . yet he bore the sin of many' (Isa. 53:12), we should not miss the point that the servant suffers *for the sake of Israel* – 'stricken for the transgression of my people' (53:8). Similarly, the cup from which Jesus recoils in Gethsemane is not simply the frightening prospect of death; it is the cup of God's anger against Jerusalem, the 'cup of staggering' that Jerusalem is made to drink (Isa. 51:17; cf. Jer. 25:15–16; Lam. 2:13 LXX; Ezek. 23:31–33). In his mind, therefore, his suffering in some sense epitomizes the brutalization of Israel under Roman rule and foreshadows the impending destruction of the city. His death on a Roman cross outside the walls of Jerusalem anticipates in a remarkably powerful fashion the punishment that would be inflicted on the Jews by Titus' soldiers. Many who sought to escape the besieged city were captured by the Romans, whipped and tortured, and then crucified in front of the city walls in the hope that the Jews would be persuaded by the horror of the spectacle to surrender. 'The soldiers themselves through rage and bitterness nailed up their victims in various attitudes as a grim joke, till owing to the vast numbers there was no room for the crosses, and no crosses for the bodies' (Jos. *J.W.* 5.11.1; cf. 2.12.6).

Raised on the third day

Daniel's vision of the turmoil that would result from Antiochus Epiphanes' assault on Judaism already goes some way toward explaining why Jesus expected the 'Son of Man' to be raised from the dead. Daniel sees a resurrection of many of those who sleep in the dust of the earth following the deliverance of Israel from pagan oppression – 'some to everlasting life, and some to shame and everlasting contempt' (Dan. 12:2).

But the reference to being raised from the dead on the 'third day' (see also Luke 24:7, 46; 1 Cor. 15:4) has its origins elsewhere. Hosea expresses as acutely as any of the Old Testament prophets the anger and ache of God's heart toward his people – the fierce repudiation of Israel and Judah because of their unfaithfulness and wickedness, and the irrepressible assurance of forgiveness. At one point he hears God say, 'I will return again to my place, until they acknowledge their guilt and seek my face, and in their distress earnestly seek me' (Hos. 5:15). His response is to call the nation to repentance: 'Come, let us return to the LORD; for he has torn us, that he may heal us; he has struck us down, and he will bind us up. After two days he will revive us; on the third day he will raise us up, that we may live before him' (Hos. 6:1–2). This is a metaphorical resurrection on the third day of a people who have suffered at the hand of God because of their sins.

So when Jesus tells his disciples that the Son of Man will be raised from the dead on the third day, he speaks about himself as suffering Israel, punished by God because of her harlotries but having the hope of forgiveness and restoration. He makes himself a parable – an embodied narrative – of what God is about to do in Israel.

The coming of the Son of Man

In much mainstream theologizing the story gets truncated at this point: he died, he rose again; believe in him and have eternal life. The vision of the Son of Man coming in his kingdom is likely to be reduced to an appendix – partly because we fear stoking up the fires of apocalyptic enthusiasm, but largely, I suspect, because we do not really know how to make sense of it. Arguably, however, the *parousia* figures more prominently in Jesus' understanding of his destiny than the resurrection. It is certainly integral to the story that is being told and must be taken with the same historical seriousness. The resurrection remains central to the witness of the early believers because it constituted the immediate experiential basis for their confidence. But the climactic moment in the eschatological narrative is the coming of the kingdom and the judgement given in favor of the Son of Man.

The transfiguration

Six days after the announcement about the suffering of the Son of Man we have the intriguing incident of the transfiguration (Matt. 17:1–13; Luke 9:28–36). Jesus takes Peter, James, and John with him up a high mountain. His appearance is transfigured, Moses and Elijah appear with him, a bright cloud overshadows them, Peter is disoriented by the whole experience, and a voice from the cloud announces, 'This is my beloved Son, with whom I am well pleased; listen to him' (Matt. 17:5; Luke 9:35).

There are several Old Testament allusions knocking around inside this passage. Moses and Elijah presumably represent the law and the prophets; the cloud that overshadows Jesus is the cloud of God's presence that overshadows the tent of meeting (cf. Exod. 40:35); and the heavenly announcement brings to mind again the conjunction of Psalm 2:7 and Isaiah 42:1 that we heard at Jesus' baptism. But the controlling Old Testament context remains the story of the Son of Man. The transfiguration follows on directly in both Matthew and Luke from Jesus' climactic assertion that within the lifetime of some of the disciples the Son of Man will be seen coming in the 'glory of his Father' (Matt. 16:27–28; Luke 9:26–27). As the group is coming down the mountain, Jesus insists that they must not tell anyone about this vision 'until the Son of Man is raised from the dead' (Matt.17:9). When the disciples are unable to heal the epileptic boy, Jesus vents his frustration with a 'faithless and twisted generation' and repeats the point that the Son of Man is about to be 'delivered into the hands of men' (Luke 9:37–44; cf. Matt. 17:22–23; Mark 9:30–32). The account of the transfiguration is locked into the Son of Man narrative.

The description of Jesus' transfigured appearance also evokes Daniel's vision of the wise who are raised following a period of extreme national tribulation and who will 'shine like the brightness of the sky above' (Dan. 12:3). It is a vision of the vindicated community of the Son of Man – the righteous, who, as Jesus has already said, will 'shine like the sun in the kingdom of their Father' when the Son of Man sends out his angels to gather the harvest at the end of the age (Matt. 13:41–43). The 'glory' that attends the 'beloved Son' in the presence of God on the mountain is the glory that the Son of Man receives from the Ancient of Days when his arch-enemy is defeated and the suffering community is vindicated (Dan. 7:14).

The transfiguration appears to be at its heart, therefore, a visual restatement of the earlier assurance that some of the disciples would live to see the disgraced, crucified Messiah publicly vindicated in the ancient world. It is not a fulfillment of that promise; it *repeats* it. The same is true of the ascension, as becomes clear when we compare it with Luke's account of the experience of the women at the tomb. When the women find that the body is missing, two men appear in 'dazzling apparel' and ask them, 'Why do you seek the living among the dead?' They remind the women that Jesus had told them while they were still in Galilee that 'the Son of Man must be delivered into the hands of sinful men and be crucified and on the third day rise' (Luke 24:4–7). Here we have the first two parts of the story of the Son of Man: suffering and resurrection. Then at the ascension two men 'in white robes' again appear and pointedly ask, 'Men of Galilee, why do you stand looking into heaven?' Luke clearly intends the reader to hear in what follows the conclusion of the story about the Son of Man: 'This Jesus, who was taken up from you into heaven, will come in the same way as you saw him go into heaven' (Acts 1:10–11). The two men do not mean that Jesus will come back to earth one day. They mean that Jesus' disappearance *into the clouds of heaven* prefigures the climactic coming of the Son of Man *on the clouds of heaven* to receive 'dominion and glory and a kingdom' from the Ancient of Days (Dan. 7:13–14). In effect, this is the answer to the disciples' question: 'Lord, will you at this time restore the kingdom to Israel?' (Acts 1:6). No, it will happen when you see the suffering community vindicated and its enemies overthrown.

The apocalyptic discourse

The prophecy that the Son of Man, who has been killed by Israel's enemies, who has been raised from the dead, will 'come with his angels in the glory of his Father' (Matt. 16:27) is repeated at the climax of Jesus' 'apocalyptic' discourse on the Mount of Olives. It is usually taken by the modern reader as a description of something that has not yet happened: the sun has not been darkened, the moon still gives its light, the stars have not fallen from heaven, and Jesus has not been seen descending to earth on the clouds with his angels to 'gather his elect from the four winds' (Matt. 24:31). I would argue, however, that the traditional 'second coming' interpretation arises from a misreading of the passage, though the case can only be outlined here.

First, the passage is quite clear about the time frame in which the events described will take place. The question that prompted the discourse in the first place assumes a close temporal connection between Jesus' 'coming,' the close of the age, and the destruction of the temple (Matt. 24:2–3). The seeing of the Son of Man coming on the clouds of heaven is said by Matthew to occur 'immediately' after the 'tribulation' of the war and is intended as a pointed contrast to the spurious hopes of deliverance offered by 'false christs and false prophets' (24:29). Jesus urges his disciples to be prepared for these events, for although he cannot tell them exactly when the war will come, he is quite clear in his insistence that 'all these things' will take place before the current generation of Jews passes away (Matt. 24:32–44). It is the same time frame that he had in mind earlier when he told his disciples that they would not have completed the task of announcing the coming of the reign of God throughout the towns of Israel 'before the Son of Man comes' (Matt. 10:23).

Secondly, the traditional interpretation misreads the apocalyptic imagery. On the one hand, the same language of cosmic collapse is used frequently in the Old Testament to signify not the literal disintegration of the cosmos but catastrophic transitions in the life of nations and empires. On the other, as I suggested at the outset, when Jesus says that the tribes of the earth will 'see' the Son of Man coming on the clouds of heaven, he means that they will see what is symbolized in Daniel's vision, namely the vindication of faithful Israel.

This brings us to the third point, which is that the story of the Son of Man has to do with the defeat of the impious and vicious forces that make war against the saints of the Most High, and with the deliverance and vindication of that suffering community. If we take seriously the historical context in which these statements are made, it is difficult to avoid the conclusion that the oppressor is the 'kings of the earth' who are gathered against the Lord and his anointed – the Jewish hierarchy, then Pontius Pilate (cf. Acts 4:26–27), then Roman imperialism, and behind these human and political enemies the power of Satan.

The story about salvation in Christ is told, therefore, as part of an eschatological narrative that has to be made sense of not mythically but *historically*, as a reading of the conflict between the righteous and the wicked in Israel, between the emerging church and its pagan environment. The Son of Man story does not simply *account for* Jesus' teaching – it establishes its frame of reference, it determines its boundaries. Within these boundaries we find the experience of those who followed him down the difficult road. The Son of Man is Jesus first, but he is also the community of those who suffered with him. This may seem a rather roundabout, obscure, and indeed gloomy journey to take in order to arrive at a compelling definition of mission for the church today. But it is the route that the early church took, and my fear is that if we attempt a short cut, we will get lost.

7

The Community of the Son of Man

For the sake of Israel Jesus has started along a difficult road, mapped in the story of the Son of Man, that will lead through suffering at the hands of Israel's enemies and eventually emerge into life. But he does not walk this road alone: he calls others to walk it with him. He forms a community around himself that shares his sense of purpose, that will drink from the same cup of God's wrath, that will be baptized with the same baptism of suffering (Mark 10:39), that will receive his Spirit, that will be known as the fellowship of his disciples, that will draw strength and inspiration from him as the branches of a vine draw life from the stem, and which will form the defining core of a restored Israel. This is the community or fellowship or brotherhood of the Son of Man – the saints of the Most High against whom the pagan oppressor makes war – whose story Jesus has pre-empted and is about to enact at the cost of his own life. He has appropriated for himself the vivid narrative of faithfulness, suffering, resurrection, and vindication, but he also openly embraces the disciples in this vision. If they are to follow him, they must be prepared to take up the cross of God's judgement against sinful Israel; if as a community they hold fast to the conviction that Jesus is indeed the one through whom God will deliver Israel from complete annihilation, then they will survive the turmoil of the end of the age, they will not be overcome by death; and when the Son of Man comes in his kingdom, they will share in his vindication and glory.

In this chapter we will consider some crucial ways in which Jesus shapes this community. First, the Sermon on the Mount in Matthew sketches the characteristics and calling of that subgroup in Israel that will choose the difficult path and find life. Secondly, this commitment on the part of the disciples is confirmed by their participation in a ritual of a renewed covenant on the basis of Jesus' death and the hope of the kingdom. Thirdly, Jesus dispatches the disciples to announce to Jews not only in Palestine but throughout the Greek–Roman world that the kingdom of God is at hand. The community of the Son of Man becomes a global movement, and the second eschatological horizon begins to come into view.

Lessons in house building

Matthew's lengthy Sermon on the Mount and Luke's much briefer Sermon on the Plain both conclude with the story of two house-builders, one wise, the other foolish (Matt. 7:24–27; Luke 6:47–49). I suggested earlier that, within the frame of reference that becomes inescapable once we begin to read historically, the storm that will batter their houses must be understood as the coming judgement on Israel – that is, the war against Rome. Undoubtedly we can draw general spiritual lessons from the parable, but Jesus' intention is quite specific: only those who put the preceding teachings into practice will survive the coming disaster. The sermon, therefore, is intended to define a community resilient enough to weather the storm.

It begins with a set of blessings or beatitudes. A beatitude is a simple statement of divine approval or favor: a man is blessed, for example, if he fears the Lord or delights in his law or does not walk in the way of the ungodly; a man is blessed 'whose transgression is forgiven, whose sin is covered' (Ps. 32:1). Jesus has adapted the form, however, for rather more programmatic and indeed subversive purposes: the beatitudes describe a marginalized and disregarded group within Israel that will benefit from some future turn of events. It is not the well-being of individuals that is at issue here: what we have in the beatitudes is a *redefinition of the true community of Israel in the light of the coming reign of God.*

This is suggested, in the first place, by the formal placement of these sayings at the head of a substantial body of teaching and by the narrative link with the initial proclamation. Jesus announces the coming of the kingdom of heaven and then defines a community of the 'poor' who will receive this kingdom. The opening statement effectively stands as a summary for everything that follows: the 'poor' in the specific eschatological sense intended here are those in Israel who mourn, who are weak, who hunger and thirst for righteousness, and so on; and their reward in various ways will be to experience the reign of God. The closing statements also reinforce the link between this group and the announcement to Israel: if as a community they make a prophetic stand for righteousness, they are bound to provoke hostility from those in power who have other interests to protect.

The real force of this connection becomes clear, however, when we follow the well-marked trails left by the beatitudes back into the dense forests of the Old Testament. The first two statements in Matthew ('Blessed are the poor in spirit, for theirs is the kingdom of heaven' and 'Blessed are those who mourn, for they shall be comforted') recall the announcement of good news to Israel in Isaiah 61:1–3: the Lord 'anointed me to bring good news to the poor . . . to comfort all who mourn.' Whether we interpret the reference to the 'poor' literally or spiritually, the announcement is made to captive Israel and has to do with a coming liberation – 'the year of the Lord's favor, and the day of vengeance of our God' (Isa. 61:2). Those who mourn are not the bereaved; nor are they people who in a more spiritual sense grieve over their personal sinfulness. They mourn *in Zion*, distressed by the wretched state of Jerusalem; they are those 'waiting for the redemption of Jerusalem' (Luke 2:38). Their comfort will be to see the restoration of Israel.

The third beatitude ('Blessed are the meek, for they shall inherit the earth') is virtually a quotation from Psalm 37:11: 'the meek shall inherit the land and delight themselves in abundant peace.' The message of the psalm is that the wicked who plot against the righteous, who 'bring down the poor and needy' and 'slay those whose way is upright' (Ps. 37:12, 14) will eventually be cut off; but the Lord will deliver those who wait on him – the poor, the oppressed, the righteous, the meek; they shall possess the land. The beatitude is not intended, therefore, as a general commendation of 'meekness' as a moral or spiritual quality: it signals a coming judgement in which the wicked will be destroyed and the oppressed will inherit the 'land' that is promised to the people of God.

Those who 'hunger and thirst for righteousness' will be 'satisfied.' The reference here is to Psalm 107, which speaks of the hungry and thirsty, whose 'soul fainted within them,' who 'cried to the LORD in their trouble': 'he satisfies the longing soul, and the hungry soul he fills with good things' (107:5–6, 9; cf. Ps. 22:26). This is not to be overspiritualized. To be satisfied is to know the faithfulness of God, who redeems from trouble and gathers the scattered in 'from the lands, from the east and from the west, from the north and from the south' (Ps. 107:2–3).

The fifth beatitude has its antecedents in Proverbs: 'the one who has mercy on the poor is most blessed' (Prov. 14:21 LXX); 'the one who has compassion shall receive mercy' (Prov. 17:5 LXX). Although the specific narrative framework is missing in this case, these statements presuppose a general background of judgement and vindication that is entirely relevant in this context: 'The wicked is overthrown through his evildoing, but the righteous finds refuge in his death' (Prov. 14:32). If 'blessed are the merciful' also has Hosea 6:6 LXX as its pre-text ('I desire mercy and not sacrifice'), the words that precede again point clearly to a context of judgement against faithless Israel: 'my judgment shall go forth as the light.'

The sixth beatitude encapsulates the promise of Psalm 24:3–6 (cf. Ps. 73:1): 'Who shall ascend the hill of the LORD? And who shall stand in his holy place? He who has clean hands and a pure heart . . . He will receive blessing from the LORD, and righteousness from the God of his salvation. Such is the generation of those who seek him, who seek the face of the God of Jacob.' In the Psalm the pure in heart, who seek God, are those who aspire to ascend the hill of the Lord and stand in his holy place. The Psalm concludes with the triumphal acclamation: 'Lift up your heads, O gates! And lift them up, O ancient doors, that the King of glory may come in.' To 'see God,' then, as the sixth beatitude has it, is to see the King of glory return to Zion, which is what Jesus will later enact with powerful prophetic symbolism when he mounts a donkey and rides into Jerusalem.

Jesus' approval of peacemakers no doubt implies *disapproval* of the activity of the militant tendency which sought to bring about the kingdom of heaven – to *save* Israel from its enemies – by violent means, and which in the end brought ruin on the nation. As Jesus warns later when Peter draws his sword in an attempt to prevent his arrest: 'all who take the sword will perish by the sword' (Matt. 26:52).

The last two beatitudes in Matthew bring into focus more sharply the suffering community: his followers will be blessed when they are 'persecuted for righteousness' sake,' when they are reviled and slandered on account of Jesus. When they suffer 'on account of the Son of Man,' as Luke has it (Luke 6:22), they become part of that community – the poor and meek who are oppressed by the wicked – and they will share in the vindication: their reward will be great in heaven, they will inherit the kingdom of God.

The statements about being salt and light that immediately follow have usually been central to definitions of the mission of the church; but they look much more at home swimming in the choppy seas of first-century Judaism than in the fish tanks of modern missiology. The eschatological community that suffers is the 'salt of the *land*' (Matt. 5:13, my translation, emphasis added). The translation highlights the narrative constrictions: there is no reason to suppose that Jesus is talking about the whole 'earth'; he means Israel. The metaphor is generally interpreted in a benign sense: the disciples are a preservative influence, or they add flavor to the meal of life. Mark, however, locates the saying about salt losing its saltiness in an argument about judgement (Mark 9:43–50). Jesus warns Israel that they would do better to cut off a hand or a foot or pluck out an eye than suffer the gehenna of God's judgement on the nation. For 'everyone will be salted with fire.' Salt that has lost its saltiness cannot be made salty again; so he tells them: 'Have salt in yourselves, and be at peace with one another.' The meaning here would appear to be that 'salt' represents the internal self-judgement that will preserve some at least in Israel from destruction. For Jesus then to say that the disciples are the 'salt of the land' suggests that the presence of the suffering community of disciples (cf. Luke 14:25–35) in Israel will be in some way a catalyst in the process of judgement and renewal. But if they lose the inner integrity of a community whose righteousness 'exceeds that of the scribes and Pharisees' (Matt. 5:20), they are 'no longer good for anything except to be thrown out and trampled under people's feet' (5:13).

When Jesus tells the disciples that they are 'the light of the world,' the image must bring to mind – if not immediately, then on reflection – Isaiah's song of the servant who would not only restore Jacob but also be given 'as a light for the nations, that my salvation may reach to the end of the earth' (Isa. 49:6; cf. 42:6). We need only hear a bar or two from a familiar song for the jukebox of memory to click into action and play it in the background of our minds. The eschatological narrative determines the meaning here. The point was made earlier when we considered Simeon's reaction to the baby in the temple that the image of Israel as 'light' in the world describes the impact that its salvation would make on the nations. Jesus' argument, therefore, is that it is in the blessed community of the righteous – through their 'good works' – that the salvation of Israel will become visible in the world, like a city on a hill or a light placed prominently in a house. If Jesus is the servant who suffers, so too are they. If he is the light of the world, so too are they. They will feel at times that they have spent their strength for nothing; but in the end they will be justified by God; their recompense is with the Lord (Isa. 49:4). They will be 'deeply despised, abhorred by the nation'; but sooner or later kings will prostrate themselves in worship because the Lord who has chosen them is faithful (49:7).

These are *eschatological* teachings: they gain their urgency and relevance from the closeness of the horizon of judgement and renewal. The law of Moses remains in force for the people of God until 'heaven and earth pass away,' until 'all is accomplished' (Matt. 5:17–18). What Jesus has in view here is not the end of the world but the moment described in the apocalyptic discourse when the Son of Man is vindicated and given the kingdom – when the old order of things passes away, when all things are accomplished (Matt. 24:34–35). If the Jews continue to harbor hatred of one another in their hearts, if they commit adultery in their hearts, if they keep the outside of the cup scrupulously clean but neglect the inside, then they will be liable to the 'gehenna of fire' (Matt. 5:21–30; cf. 23:25–26). The disciples should not hate the enemies who oppress the righteous in Israel: they should love them. We saw earlier that the prayer Jesus taught them is a prayer for the restoration of Israel and the vindication of the community that trusts in the Father. Israel is on a broad path leading to the destruction of war, when 'Every tree . . . that does not bear good fruit is cut down and thrown into the fire' (Matt. 3:10), when a flood will destroy the city and the sanctuary.

The new covenant in his sufferings

What most clearly identifies the disciples as a community that will share in the sufferings of the Son of Man is the informal ritual that Jesus initiated at the Last Supper. The disciples have been fashioned into a new Israel. Jesus' death is the basis for the 'new covenant' that binds them together. Whenever they break the bread and drink the cup, they are reminded of the fact that they must make the long exodus from oppression to creational renewal not according to the terms of the old covenant but by taking the difficult road of faithfulness through suffering to vindication. This is why the meal has in view the coming of the kingdom (Luke 22:18). The Son of Man who is betrayed and goes to his death will receive the kingdom from the Ancient of Days; and those who are united with him by covenant in his death will feast with him (the symbolism of the meal naturally carries over) in the Father's kingdom.

Jesus' argument with the Jews in John 6 supports this. The fathers ate manna in the wilderness to keep them alive on their arduous journey from slavery to the land that had been promised to them. For Israel to 'live' during the new exodus that it must undertake, it must – so to speak – eat Jesus himself: 'I am the living bread that came down from heaven. If anyone eats of this bread, he will live for ever. And the bread that I will give for the life of the world is my flesh' (John 6:51). The Jews are mystified by this, so Jesus explains: whoever eats the flesh and drinks the blood of the Son of Man will have the life of the age to come; Jesus will 'raise him up on the last day' (6:54). This is how they will make the journey from oppression to renewal – by identifying themselves in a very concrete way with the one who suffers for the sake of Israel and is vindicated.

It is entirely right in this connection to stress that there was for Israel *only one path* that would lead to life. Jesus' claim in John 14:6 to be 'the way, the truth, and the life,' the only means of access to the Father, is spoken in the context of a difficult and confused conversation with the disciples about his imminent death. Judas has left the meal to betray Jesus to the Jewish authorities. Jesus tells the others that the time has come for the Son of Man to be glorified, and we should hear in this, I think, a deliberate allusion to the drama of Daniel 7 in which the figure coming with the clouds to receive 'dominion and glory and a kingdom' represents the oppressed saints of the Most High. He adds that they cannot follow him where he is going at this point, but they will follow afterward – indeed, he will come and take them with him to his Father's house where rooms are prepared for them. When he suggests that they know the 'way' to this place, Thomas expresses surprise: 'Lord, we do not know where you are going. How can we know the way?' The destination is to be with the Father; the way is the path of suffering that Jesus is about to walk, but because the Son of Man motif is in the background, we easily understand that it is a path that his disciples will also have to follow sooner or later: they are, in Jesus' reworking of the vision, the saints of the Most High who will suffer and be glorified in the presence of the Father. The exclusivist claim, therefore, is that only by taking the path of faithful suffering that Jesus has conceived for himself will oppressed Israel be vindicated and glorified in the presence of the Father. All other roads lead to Rome.

Fishers of men

The image of fields white for the harvest has been a perennial inspiration to mission, and Jesus' exhortation to pray that God will send out more laborers into the harvest has provided a central paradigm for modern missionary activity (Matt. 9:37–38; Luke 10:2; John 4:35). Mission means raising up more missionaries to go out into the world to convert the large numbers of people who supposedly are waiting to be converted. But we need to stay on the path of the narrative. Or narratives. In Matthew the saying comes as a response to the sight of the crowds who were 'harassed and helpless, like sheep without a shepherd' (Matt. 9:36). In Luke it forms part of Jesus' instructions to the larger group of seventy-two disciples when he sends them out ahead of him to tell people that the 'kingdom of God has come near to you' (Luke 10:9).

When Jesus calls the fishermen Simon and Andrew to follow him, he tells them that he will make them 'fishers of men' (Mark 1:17; Matt. 4:19). His words may carry a memory of Jeremiah's disturbing image of YHWH sending for 'many fishers' to gather the people of Israel in order to 'hurl' them out of the land as punishment for their idolatry (Jer. 16:16), but the sense is rather different. The task of the disciples will be to save people from destruction. In Luke's account the invitation is preceded by the story of how Jesus instructed Simon to let down his nets into the Sea of Galilee. When the nets come up breaking under the weight of fish, Simon is astounded, but Jesus tells him, 'Do not be afraid; from now on you will be catching men' (Luke 5:10). The word for 'catching' (*zōgran*) strongly suggests the idea of keeping alive or sparing captives (e.g. Josh. 9:20; 2 Sam. 8:2; 2 Chr. 25:12 LXX). The disciples will 'save' people from the coming judgement on Israel.

Jesus sends them out simply to do what he himself has been doing. They are the faithful community of the Son of Man. They have the same authority to heal the sick, raise the dead, cleanse lepers, and cast out unclean spirits – an authority given in advance for the sake of the prophetic proclamation that the kingdom of God is at hand. They are to go only to the 'lost sheep of the house of Israel' with the announcement that 'the kingdom of heaven is at hand' (Matt. 10:1, 5–8).

For some this will be a message of peace. There is no calling to follow, no making of disciples, no planting of churches. The disciples simply leave behind individuals, families, communities, who will wait patiently for God to act on behalf of Israel. But for those who do not welcome them, who do not offer them hospitality, who refuse to listen to what they have to say, the outcome will be grim: 'it will be more bearable on the day of judgement for the land of Sodom and Gomorrah than for that town' (10:15). When we read this, we should think of a murderous army passing through Galilee on its way to Jerusalem, ransacking and burning the homes of a stubborn population that refused to take the option of peace. That will be their day of judgement, and it is not so far away.

As the Son of Man community, the disciples can expect to be opposed – as sheep in the midst of wolves. They will be hated, vilified, ostracized, rejected by their own communities, betrayed by family and friends, arrested, condemned, imprisoned. The prospect of families being torn apart by the deeply antisocial actions of the disciples is realistic enough, but it is also a sign. Jesus clearly recalls Micah's narrative of judgement against Jerusalem, when 'the son treats the father with contempt, the daughter rises up against her mother, the daughter-in-law against her mother-in-law; a man's enemies are the men of his own house' (Mic. 7:6). The allusion reinforces the historical frame of reference for Jesus' instructions: 'the LORD has an indictment against his people, and he will contend with Israel' (6:2).

But when the disciples stand before their accusers and judges, they will know what to say because they will have the same Spirit – and therefore the same *spirit*, the same mind, the same attitude, the same hope – as the one who will soon stand before both the Jewish council and the Roman governor. If at that moment they acknowledge Jesus, the Son of Man will acknowledge them before the angels of God, before the throne of the Ancient of Days (Luke 12:8). If they remain faithful through all the suffering, they will survive; not a hair of their heads will perish, they will gain their lives (Luke 21:18–19).

How long will it take? Jesus is quite clear: 'you will not have gone through all the towns of Israel before the Son of Man comes' (Matt. 10:23). He is speaking about a foreseeable future that belongs to the restoration of Israel. Jesus later assures the disciples that in his kingdom, in the 'regeneration,' 'when the Son of Man will sit on his glorious throne, you who have followed me will also sit on twelve thrones, judging the twelve tribes of Israel' (Matt. 19:28; Luke 22:30). 'Regeneration' is *palingenesia* (ESV has 'new world''). In the background is Isaiah's use of the metaphor of new creation to describe the restoration of Israel (Isa. 65:17; 66:22). Josephus uses the word to refer to the 'rebirth' of the nation following the exile (*Ant.* 11.2.9 §66).

Before the end comes, however, the gospel of the kingdom will have been 'proclaimed throughout the whole world as a testimony to all nations' (Matt. 24:14). The task of the disciples is not only to announce the coming of judgement and salvation in the towns and villages of Israel. Something is to be announced throughout the world. But what? And to what end?

The risen Jesus explains to the two disciples over dinner in Emmaus: 'Thus it is written, that the Christ should suffer and on the third day rise from the dead, and that repentance and forgiveness of sins should be proclaimed in his name to all nations, beginning from Jerusalem. You are witnesses of these things' (Luke 24:46–48). An exhortation to global evangelism? Well, yes, in a sense, but we need to explain what we mean by this. For the 'good news' that is declared to all nations in the name of the Son of Man who suffered and rose on the third day *still has to do essentially with what God has done for Israel*: it is that a section of Israel at least has turned back from its self-destructive course and found forgiveness from the sins that brought judgement. When God acts on behalf of his people Israel, the news is proclaimed throughout the world: 'Go out from Babylon, flee from Chaldea, declare this with a shout of joy, proclaim it, send it out to the end of the earth; say, "The LORD has redeemed his servant Jacob!" ' (Isa. 48:20; cf. 62:11). We are still hiking across the hilly landscape of the narrative with its restricted view of the future. Peter's words in Acts 5:31–32, which closely parallel what Jesus says in Luke 24:46–49, make this abundantly clear: 'God exalted him at his right hand as Leader and Saviour, to give repentance to Israel and forgiveness of sins. And we are witnesses to these things, and so is the Holy Spirit, whom God has given to those who obey him.'

To the end of the age . . .

Matthew constructs the final charge to the disciples rather differently:

> And Jesus came and said to them, 'All authority in heaven and on earth has been given to me. Go therefore and make disciples of all nations, baptizing them in the name of the Father and of the Son and of the Holy Spirit, teaching them to observe all that I have commanded you. And behold, I am with you always, to the end of the age.' (Matt. 28:18–20)

Probably more than any other statement in the New Testament this commission has defined the central task given to the church. But the question we should ask first is, What is this 'age'? And more to the point, When will it come to an end? In other words, what is the *eschatological* time frame within which the mission of the disciples as it is conceived here will take place?

We need to rewind the tape a bit. A few days earlier as Jesus was leaving the temple with his disciples, he must have astonished them with his stark prediction that this place of God's dwelling, this overblown centerpiece of Israel's faith, this stunning monument to Herod's political ambitions, this fortress for the preservation of Israel's ancestral traditions and the interests of Jerusalem's political elite, would be razed to the ground. Not one stone would be left upon another. The small group walked across the valley of Kidron and found a spot on the Mount of Olives from where they could look back at the temple. Not surprisingly the disciples were curious to know when this calamity would strike: 'Tell us, when will these things be, and what will be the sign of your coming and of the close of the age?' (Matt. 24:3). The assumption that they make is quite clear: the destruction of the temple would coincide with the 'coming' or *parousia* of Jesus and the 'close of the age.'

I have looked at this assumption at length in *The Coming of the Son of Man*. We will also come back to it later in this book. For now I simply suggest that when Jesus speaks of being with his disciples 'all the days until the completion of the age' (my translation), he is thinking specifically of the period leading up to the final collapse of second-temple Judaism – in other words, up to the wrong-headed uprising against Rome and the destruction of Jerusalem in AD 70. We need to contract the thought down to relevant and historical proportions: we are still in this mentally cramped, rabbit-hole world. Jesus sends the disciples out to confront a state of crisis – a protracted state of crisis, admittedly, but not an unbounded one.

The significance of the assurance lies in the fact that he knows they will have to endure the same hostility and abuse during this period that he himself is about to go through. The apocalyptic drama of the Son of Man is faintly in the background, but the Son of Man is a symbolic figure who represents the saints of the Most High who suffer because Israel is oppressed by a violent and blasphemous pagan enemy. When the disciples find themselves handed over to courts, flogged in the synagogues, and dragged before Gentile rulers (cf. Matt. 10:16–18), when they are delivered up to tribulation, put to death, hated by all nations because of the Christ (Matt. 24:9), they share in the sufferings of Jesus. He is the Son of Man who has prefigured their sufferings in his own; and in imitating him they manifest *his Spirit*, they demonstrate the fact that he is with them – and will be with them every day as long as this state of affairs prevails.

The emphasis in this closing injunction is not, as in Luke, on the announcement about the salvation of Israel but on the formation of a global community. The reference to the 'authority' that has been given to Jesus sets this within the story about the Son of Man, who is given an 'authority which might not be taken away and his kingdom which might not be destroyed' (Dan. 7:14 LXX, my translation). Under this authority they are to make disciples – men and women who will learn from them what it means to be counted among the oppressed saints of the Most High as they make their way along the difficult road that leads to life. As a result of their obedience to the teaching of Jesus they will constitute a community that will survive the birth pangs of the age to come. So when he instructs them to baptize these new believers 'in the name of the Father and of the Son and of the Holy Spirit' (Matt. 28:19), we should probably hear in these words not an abstract Trinitarian formula but a precise encapsulation of the eschatological *narrative* about suffering and renewal. They are baptized in the name of the Father who chooses a community to make the treacherous journey, of the Son who anticipates in his own journey their suffering and their hope of vindication, and of the Spirit of prophecy which, as we shall see in the next chapter, is to be poured out in the 'last days.'

The prophet Jesus, like John the Baptist before him, saw judgement coming on a sinful, rebellious, hypocritical people. That is the theological analysis. It corresponds to a political insight – that sooner or later the Jews would start a fight with Rome and lose it badly. The outcome would be an end to the temple system, the land, and any semblance of self-government as a nation. The *only hope* he saw was to create around himself an alternative faithful, justified Israel, which would walk the narrow road leading eventually to life. This is how Israel would be saved – not by violence, not by meretricious collaboration with the oppressor, not by pious isolationism, not by appealing to covenantal prerogatives, not even by 'faith' as some sort of abstract spiritual exploit or virtue, but by the faithful participation of the *Christ-like* community in the story of the Son of Man.

In the process, Jesus fell victim to the destruction that would soon come on the whole nation: he was destroyed by Rome, by the blunt instrument of God's wrath. He suffered the historical 'punishment' that was Israel's, but it meant that the people would continue, centered around the temple of his body, inheriting the whole world (cf. Rom. 4:13) and not just the land of Canaan, and with Christ himself as king. Now we can take this argument on into Luke's account of the early years of the church. What did it mean for renewed Israel to inherit the world?

8

What Happens when the Good News is Announced in the Pagan World

According to conventional wisdom the Gospels tell the story of the foundational saving event – Jesus' death and resurrection – and Luke's second historical work, the book of Acts, tells the story of the expansion of the church, beginning with the outpouring of the Spirit at Pentecost. We might call this the inflationary model of mission: there is a balloon in the room which starts very small but gets bigger and bigger until eventually it fills all available space, at which point the balloon bursts, the house falls down, and we all go to heaven.

Under the régime of Christendom the model remained more or less plausible. But the balloon was badly damaged by the Enlightenment and in the Western half of the room, at least, is still losing air at an alarming rate. It has pushed up against large, immovable cultural and intellectual objects, some of them quite sharp – religions, belief systems, ideologies – and it's not at all clear that it can make further progress. This is the crisis of modernism. We are having to ask serious questions about what the balloon is doing in the room. Is it really supposed to occupy the entire space of human existence? What if it was only ever meant to be a lovely red balloon, filled with the helium of the Holy Spirit, just floating there for everyone to see?

The argument here will be that the central missional theme of Acts is essentially the same as that of the Gospels: the announcement of the reign of God to Israel within an eschatological horizon defined by the prospect of impending judgement – that is, by the prospect of a disastrous war against Rome. The difference, in the first place, is that the announcement is made not only to the inhabitants of Jerusalem and Judea but to *diaspora* Israel – to the scattered Jews who would be gathered and brought back to the homeland at the end of the age. Secondly, however, the preaching of the gospel of the kingdom in the Gentile world is to have consequences that will certainly take the disciples by surprise and which are not clearly foreseen in Jesus' instructions.

So while it is true that there is a powerful centrifugal movement in Acts that threatens to overwhelm its eschatological container, we still need to read the book as part of a narrative that does not quite reach its climax. The temple system remains in place; the fate of Judaism is still in the hands of the various factions vying for influence in Jerusalem; Rome is still the overlord – threatening, brutal, sometimes judicious, sometimes quite monstrous in its arrogant disregard for the religious sensibilities of the Jews.

Luke tells us that in the period between the resurrection and the ascension Jesus appeared to the disciples on a number of occasions and spoke to them about the kingdom of God. This is the same 'kingdom of God' that he had announced throughout Galilee and Judea: within a generation God would bring Israel's state of condemnation to a climax, the old order of things would be swept away, its enemies would be defeated, a new creational microcosm would emerge, differentiated from other cultures and nations by the Spirit of the living God in its midst, and those who had to share in Christ's sufferings would be vindicated.

If the disciples recalled all this, or if it had formed part of what the risen Jesus taught them, the question naturally occurs to them: 'Lord, will you at this time restore the kingdom to Israel?' (Acts 1:6). They are like impatient children in the back of the car on their way to the seaside: 'Are we there yet? Are we there yet?' His answer is oblique, if not evasive, but he does not suggest that it was an unreasonable or inappropriate question to ask: it was not for them to know 'times or seasons that the Father has fixed by his own authority,' but they would receive power when the Holy Spirit came upon them and would be his witnesses 'in Jerusalem and in all Judea and Samaria, and to the end of the earth' (Acts 1:6–8). He refuses to be specific about the time, but he does not correct the basic assumption – a matter of historical relevance – that this generation of Jews, or perhaps their children, would see the restoration of the kingdom to Israel. What we have here, in fact, is a condensed version of Jesus' apocalyptic discourse, when the disciples earlier put to him a question about timing: when will the temple be destroyed, when will the *parousia* happen, when will be the end of the age (Matt. 24:3; Mark 13:4)? Jesus cannot give them the day or hour (Matt. 24:36; Mark 13:32), but he can give them an impressionistic prophetic account of the events that will culminate in the coming of the Son of Man on the clouds of heaven to receive an everlasting kingdom on behalf of righteous Israel.

So when he tells the disciples that they will be his witnesses to the ends of the earth, it must have something to do with the expectation that the kingdom will be restored to Israel *within the temporal framework established in the apocalyptic discourse*. They are to travel out from Jerusalem and tell the Jews of the Diaspora that judgement is coming to a climax, the ax is laid to the root of the trees, the harvest is approaching, the net will soon be brought in and the fish sorted, the flood waters are rising; and that the kingdom will be given to that part of Israel which faithfully endures suffering, which trusts in the way of the Christ. For the disciples this expectation is well grounded. They have seen the risen Lord. They know that the dangerous path of faithful obedience does not end in death and decay: God has not abandoned his soul to Hades, he has not allowed his holy one to see corruption (cf. Acts 2:27).

Luke's narrative, therefore, begins with a quite emphatic statement about the kingdom of God: the disciples will go out from Jerusalem to announce to Jewish communities of the Diaspora, throughout the Greek–Roman world, that the reign of God is not far off. It is an announcement to Israel at this stage (cf. Acts 11:19; 13:5) for the simple reason that it is a message *about Israel*. In a sense, it is none of the Gentiles' business. But first Pentecost.

Save yourselves from this crooked generation

When Peter addresses the bemused throng which has gathered around the house on the day of Pentecost, he interprets the peculiar agitation of the disciples as a fulfillment of words spoken by the prophet Joel. In the last days God will pour out his Spirit on all people in Israel, men and women, young and old, freeborn and slaves. This extravagant and indiscriminate experience of the Spirit certainly marks a radical transformation of the spiritual life of the people: it is a sign of forgiveness and renewal (cf. Ezek. 36:26–27). But it is also a Spirit of prophecy: 'your sons and your daughters shall prophesy, and your young men shall see visions, and your old men shall dream dreams; even on my male servants and female servants in those days I will pour out my Spirit, and they shall prophesy' (Acts 2:17–18). This needs to be understood in a quite specific sense: *many* in Israel – not just a handful of recognized prophets but a diverse, expanding community – are gaining the prophetic insight into what God is about to do.

There is a disturbing side to Joel's vision that generally gets overlooked in our happy-go-lucky charismatic enthusiasm but which situates Pentecost firmly within the eschatological narrative of first-century Judaism. The giving of the Spirit would be accompanied by 'wonders in the heavens above and signs on the earth below, blood, and fire, and vapor of smoke; the sun shall be turned to darkness and the moon to blood, before the day of the Lord comes, the great and magnificent day' (Acts 2:19–20). In Joel's prophetic imagination this would be a day of devastation for Jerusalem ('magnificent' in the ESV is not a good translation), from which only those who called on the name of the Lord would escape (Joel 2:32), because the people of Judah 'have shed innocent blood in their land' (3:19). 'For the day of the LORD is great and very awesome; who can endure it?' (Joel 2:11).

The conclusion we are bound to draw is that for Peter the remarkable events of the day of Pentecost are a sign to his audience that a similar day of devastation is not far off. The salvation that he holds out to them, therefore, is precisely escape from *national* disaster. When he urges them to save themselves from 'this crooked generation,' to repent and be baptized for the forgiveness of their sins (Acts 2:38–40), he is doing what John the Baptist did earlier: he is calling the people of Jerusalem to repentance because the ax is already laid to the root of the trees. When he quotes Moses' warning concerning a future prophet that 'every soul who does not listen to that prophet shall be destroyed from the people,' he means it quite literally: if they refuse to take the difficult path of obedience, they will be slaughtered.

The parallelism is precise and no doubt deliberate. The multitudes earlier came to John asking, 'What then shall we do?' (Luke 3:10). The crowds now come to Peter and the apostles asking, 'Brothers, what shall we do?' (Acts 2:37). They are not looking for personal salvation. They are asking what they *as Israel* must do to survive the wrath of God that will consume the nation. The believers who are baptized, who devote themselves to the apostles' teaching and fellowship, who break bread together, who sell their possessions and distribute the money to those who have need, who go to the temple daily, who eat together joyfully, who praise God and who find favor with all the people, are 'those who were being saved' – not because they all now have the assurance that they will go to heaven but because they comprise a community within Israel that will not be destroyed on the great and terrible day of the Lord (Acts 2:41–47).

The argument is heard again in Peter's speech following the healing of the lame man at the temple gate.

> Repent therefore, and turn again, that your sins may be blotted out, that times of refreshing may come from the presence of the Lord, and that he may send the Christ appointed for you, Jesus, whom heaven must receive until the time for restoring all the things about which God spoke by the mouth of his holy prophets long ago. (Acts 3:19–21)

It is *Jacob* whose transgressions are blotted out like a cloud (Isa. 44:22); it is *Israel* whose wickedness will be blotted out after centuries of exile (Dan. 9:24 Theodotion). The 'times of refreshing' are a respite from the state of spiritual confusion and oppression that will come to an end at the coming of the Christ and the restoration of all things. This restoration of all things prophesied in Scripture is the restoration of the kingdom to Israel that the disciples asked Jesus about.

The argument is also heard in Peter's defense before the rulers and elders of Israel. The stone which the builders rejected has become the head of the corner. There is no other hope for salvation, 'no other name under heaven given among men by which we must be saved' (Acts 4:11–12). The image comes from Psalm 118:22. Jesus used it in effect as a summary of the parable of the vineyard and its tenants: Israel rejects the owner's son, but he becomes the head of the corner, and 'Everyone who falls on that stone will be broken to pieces, and when it falls on anyone, it will crush him' (Luke 20:17–18; cf. Matt. 21:42–43; Mark 12:10–11). For Peter, too, it is a commentary on the spiritual condition of the rulers and elders of Israel. If they reject the way of peace, the city will be destroyed. There is no alternative – no other name by which Israel will be saved. Again, the exclusivist force of the assertion must be heard, but it must be heard within the narrative: the only hope for Israel is to trust the announcement that God has raised Jesus from the dead.

The political orientation of the controversy is illustrated by Gamaliel's pragmatic judgement following the escape of the apostles from prison. He reminds the council of two revolutionary movements that were ruthlessly suppressed by the Romans and offers the following advice: 'keep away from these men and let them alone, for if this plan or this undertaking is of man, it will fail; but if it is of God, you will not be able to overthrow them. You might even be found opposing God!' (Acts 5:38–39). He clearly regards the movement to be pursuing a similar purpose or plan to that of the failed insurrectionaries: that is, to save oppressed Israel from the rule of Rome, to overcome the enemies of Israel. What we should note is that apparently he reaches this conclusion after hearing Peter accuse the council of having killed Jesus, whom God has now exalted 'as Leader and Savior, to give repentance to Israel and forgiveness of sins' (5:31). He may have misunderstood the *means* of this salvation, but he was certainly right to see that they presented a serious challenge to the political status quo.

Paul and the hope of Israel

What Peter declares in Jerusalem, Paul announces to the Jews of the Diaspora. Invited to speak in the synagogue in Pisidian Antioch, he argues that Jesus was the promised descendant of David who would save Israel, the family of Abraham (Acts 13:23, 26). The general argument here still does not allow us to introduce the thought of a universal personal salvation: Jesus is *Israel's* savior within a particular narrative of judgement.

John the Baptist, Paul argues, called the people of Jerusalem and Judea to repentance in order to escape the coming wrath; but his preaching could only be a prelude to the coming of one who would baptize with the Holy Spirit and with fire, who would clear the threshing floor of Israel, gathering the wheat into his granary and burning the chaff with the 'unquenchable fire' of God's judgement (Luke 3:16–17). The rulers of Jerusalem condemned this 'savior' and had him killed, but by raising him from the dead God fulfilled the promise to the fathers that new life would come from the devastation of judgement. So Paul makes it clear to his Jewish audience: the forgiveness of Israel's sins is announced through this man, and in him everyone who believes is justified from everything that they could not be justified from by the law of Moses (Acts 13:38–39). To underline the seriousness of this claim he quotes from Habakkuk 1:5 LXX: 'Look, you scoffers, be astounded and perish; for I am doing a work in your days, a work that you will not believe, even if one tells it to you.' This is no vacuous warning. Habakkuk foresaw the coming of the invading Chaldean army (Hab. 1:6). Paul must have imagined a similar fate for Israel: a powerful and brutal nation, ordained by God as a judgement and reproof (cf. Hab. 1:12), would march into Judea bringing destruction upon those who scoffed at the message of salvation. We will have more to say on this whole theme later when we listen to the story that Paul tells in Romans.

In the end the Jews of Pisidian Antioch reject this argument about judgement and the forgiveness of Israel's sins – as Paul ironically puts it, they judge themselves 'unworthy of eternal life' (Acts 13:46). So Paul and Barnabas turn to the Gentiles. When eventually they are hounded out of the Jewish district, they shake off the dust from their feet as a sign that the reign of God has come near (Acts 13:51). The gesture symbolizes God's rejection of his people, whether they are in Galilee, Samaria, Judea (Luke 9:5; 10:11; cf. Matt. 10:14; Mark 6:11), or the cities of the Greek–Roman world.

In the later chapters in Acts, Paul has to defend himself before various tribunals against accusations made by the Jews. He is quite clear about the central matter of dispute: 'It is with respect to the hope of the resurrection of the dead that I am on trial' (Acts 23:6). The point is made repeatedly in these speeches: he has a hope in God that 'there will be a resurrection of both the just and the unjust' (24:15); it is 'with respect to the resurrection of the dead' that he is on trial (24:21); he is 'on trial because of my hope in the promise made by God to our fathers, to which our twelve tribes hope to attain' (26:6). We can neither privatize nor universalize this hope: it is the hope of *national* resurrection at a time of judgement.

Paul's argument at Pisidian Antioch is that in some sense this *national* hope has been fulfilled or anticipated in the raising of Jesus from the dead: 'we bring you the good news that what God promised to the fathers, this he has fulfilled to us their children by raising Jesus' (Acts 13:32–33). But the premature raising of Jesus from the dead remains part of the narrative about judgement on Israel. The resurrection of the just and the unjust is the resurrection that Daniel foresees, when Israel will be delivered after a period of unprecedented suffering (Dan. 12:2). The righteous who will be raised on that day of deliverance are the 'wise among the people,' who know their God; they will stand firm against the king who 'shall exalt himself and magnify himself above every god, and shall speak astonishing things against the God of gods' (Dan. 11:32–33, 36). They are also, therefore, in Daniel's multilayered apocalyptic narrative, the saints of the Most High against whom the little horn makes war but who receive an everlasting kingdom

(Dan. 7:21–27). The community that is raised is – quite narrowly – the community that suffers. We see the same thing in the Old Testament text that speaks of a resurrection on the third day. Hosea articulates the hope of suffering Ephraim, torn and struck down by the Lord: 'After two days he will revive us; on the third day he will raise us up, that we may live before him' (Hos. 6:2).

The significance of this connection between the suffering of God's people and resurrection becomes apparent when we notice that at the heart of Paul's defense both before Felix and before Festus and King Agrippa is a story about persecution. In his zeal for the law Paul 'persecuted this Way to the death' – arresting and imprisoning many of the saints, casting his vote against them when they were put to death, punishing them in the synagogues, trying to make them blaspheme (Acts 22:4–5, 19; 26:10–11). On a journey to Damascus to hunt down more of these sectarians, he has some sort of visionary encounter with the risen Christ, who identifies himself as 'Jesus of Nazareth whom you are persecuting' (22:8; cf. 26:14–15). The risen Christ *is* the suffering community – just as Isaiah's servant is wounded and bruised Israel, just as the Son of Man is the people of the saints of the Most High, just as Jesus himself is encountered in his brethren when they are hungry, thirsty, rejected, naked, sick, imprisoned (Matt. 25:35–40).

Light to the Gentiles

The mission to the Gentiles in Acts is an outworking of the salvation of Israel. When the Jews in Pisidian Antioch refuse to believe the announcement that 'what God promised to the fathers, this he has fulfilled to us their children by raising Jesus,' that forgiveness of sins has been declared through this man, that the possibility has emerged of escaping the judgement that the law prescribes, Paul and Barnabas turn to the Gentiles. To justify their action they cite Isaiah 49:6: 'I have made you a light for the Gentiles, that you may bring salvation to the ends of the earth' (Acts 13:46–47; cf. 28:28). But this remains part of God's agenda for Israel. It is an appeal to the servant story. The servant was 'deeply despised, abhorred by the nation' (Isa. 49:7). He has been helped 'in a day of salvation' (49:8). He appears to have 'labored in vain' but his 'right is with the LORD'; he is 'honored in the eyes of the LORD' (49:4–5). He will be used to 'raise up the tribes of Jacob and to bring back the preserved of Israel,' and as such he has been given as a 'light for the nations, that my salvation may reach to the end of the earth' (49:6). Then kings and princes will come and prostrate themselves before the formerly despised servant 'because of the LORD, who is faithful, the Holy One of Israel, who has chosen you' (49:7). The mission to the Gentiles, undertaken by the servant community, is a mission to make known what God has done for his afflicted and impoverished people.

The Gentiles 'hear the word of the gospel and believe' (Acts 15:7): that is, they believe the announcement that God has redeemed Israel through Jesus; this belief in God finds expression first in repentance and secondly in worship through the power of the Spirit; through the work of the Spirit they become part of the worshiping community; and this participation, finally, is ratified through baptism into the story of the Son of Man. The Lord has in this way 'visited the Gentiles, to take from them a people for his name' (15:14). Israel is restored as a hybrid community consisting of a remnant of the people and 'all the Gentiles who are called by my name' (15:17). James has constructed this argument from Amos 9:8–12 LXX. The eyes of the Lord are on the sinful kingdom of Israel; the nation will be erased from the face of the earth, but not all will die; the sinners will be destroyed by the sword, but in that day of judgement God will restore Israel's place of worship, so that 'the remnant of the people may seek the Lord, and all the Gentiles who are called by my name' (Acts 15:16–17, my translation).

What makes the inclusion of Gentiles in the people of God an act of *salvation* and not merely of blessing is, first, the fact that the ancient world is under divine judgement because of idolatry. Just as Peter urged the people of Jerusalem to save themselves from a 'crooked generation' that was heading for catastrophe (Acts 2:40), so Paul insists that Greek and Roman society faces a judgement from which they will not be saved by their idols (Acts 17:29–31; cf. 14:15–17). The God who made the world and everything in it, the Lord of heaven and earth, who made every nation with the intention that they should seek God, feel their way toward him and find him, is no longer willing to overlook their ignorance. He commands not just Israel to repent of its wickedness and unfaithfulness but also the pagan world to repent of its idolatry and the immorality and injustice that flow from it.

This provokes both a political and a religious crisis. On the one hand, the Jews in Thessalonica drag Jason and others of the brethren before the city authorities complaining that 'they are all acting against the decrees of Caesar, saying that there is another king, Jesus' (Act 17:7). On the other, the silversmith Demetrius protests that 'not only in Ephesus but in almost all of Asia this Paul has persuaded and turned away a great many people, saying that gods made with hands are not gods' (Acts 19:26). But when Paul says that God has determined a day on which he will judge the Greek–Roman world 'in righteousness by a man whom he has appointed' (Acts 17:31), the language invokes an argument from the Psalms. Psalm 98, for example, speaks of the Lord's vindication of 'the house of Israel' in the sight of the nations and calls the whole earth to rejoice on behalf of this salvation because the Lord comes to judge the earth: 'He will judge the world with righteousness, and the peoples with equity' (Ps. 98:9). This is not an end-of-history judgement. It is judgement on a civilization or culture at a certain moment in history, first, because that civilization or culture is idolatrous, and secondly, because it aggressively opposes the people of God.

Similarly, when Paul reports of the believers in Thessalonica that they 'turned to God from idols to serve the living and true God, and to wait for his Son from heaven, whom he raised from the dead, Jesus who delivers us from the wrath to come' (1 Thess. 1:9–10), he is thinking not of a final judgement but of judgement on the pagan civilization that opposes the people of God. The idolatrous Greek–Roman world will be challenged and eventually defeated by communities of the Son of Man that remain steadfast in the face of persecution as they proclaim that Jesus Christ is Lord, that he has been given the name which is above every name. In the end, even the reigning metanarrative of Roman imperialism will be silenced.

Secondly, Gentiles are 'saved' in the sense that they have been included in a community that has entered into the life of the age to come (Acts 13:46, 48). As Peter learned at Caesarea, there is no obstacle to membership of the community of Israel forgiven and restored. This is utterly new. It is the mystery that was made known to Paul by revelation, which was 'not made known to the sons of men in other generations as it has now been revealed to his holy apostles and prophets by the Spirit' – that 'the Gentiles are fellow heirs, members of the same body, and partakers of the promise in Christ Jesus through the gospel' (Eph. 3:3–6). By the grace of God and through faith in the story about Jesus, Gentiles become part of a community that will inherit in the coming ages the promise of creational blessing given to Abraham (Eph. 2:8–9).

Peter's revolutionary and controversial insight is that there either is no longer or never has been a valid division in God's eyes between Jews and Gentiles *as a matter of ritual cleanness*. This is what the test case of Cornelius proved. It may be *unlawful* for a Jew to associate with a Gentile but, Peter says, 'God has shown me that I should not call any person common or unclean'; 'God shows no partiality' (Acts 10:28, 34). So a Roman such as Cornelius is not automatically barred from inclusion in the fellowship of God's people simply on the grounds that he is an unclean foreigner and not a circumcised descendant of Abraham. But there is a qualification: 'in every nation anyone who fears him and does what is right is acceptable to him' (10:35). The point here is that Cornelius' piety and righteousness, as evidenced by the fact that he fears God, gives alms generously and prays continually (10:2), constitute for him the 'fruit in keeping with repentance' that is required of sinful Israel. Therefore, he is 'saved' – in the sense that he has become part of a resilient community of refugees that must pick its way through the war zone of eschatological transition in hope of reaching a new existence in the age to come (11:14, 18). Peter relates the story about Jesus, which is 'good news of peace' for Israel, concluding with the affirmation that Jesus has been appointed judge of the living and the dead and that every one who believes receives 'forgiveness of sins through his name' (10:36–43). Immediately the Spirit falls on the gathered Gentiles, much to the astonishment of the Jewish believers present.

When Peter later has to defend himself against criticism from the circumcision party in Jerusalem, he suggests that what happened was a fulfillment of Jesus' words, 'John baptized with water, but you will be baptized with the Holy Spirit' (11:16; cf. 1:5). Just as repentant Israel was baptized by John with water, so repentant Gentiles are baptized with the Holy Spirit (11:16). The apostles and brethren draw the conclusion: 'Then to the Gentiles also God has granted repentance that leads to life' (11:18). But this is not a spiritual life independent of the story about Israel: it is the life of renewed Israel.

Eschatological communities

The disciples are told that they will receive the power of the eschatological Spirit, poured out in the first place to enable the church to bear witness prophetically to the coming judgement on Israel, the renewal of God's people, and the eventual vindication of those who suffer. Then they will be his witnesses within the eschatological horizon determined by the coming of the Son of Man. That is, they will be witnesses within the geographical and temporal sphere of the rule of Caesar, announcing 'in Jerusalem and in all Judea and Samaria, and to the end of the earth' that Jesus has been exalted to the right hand of God in the manner described in Psalm 110 as Lord and Christ until all his enemies have been defeated (Acts 2:33–36).

So what we see emerging in Acts are Christ-like communities, assemblies of the Son of Man, designed to survive the wrath coming on both Israel and the Greek–Roman world because the stone which the leaders in Jerusalem rejected as a futile and dangerous distraction has become the head of the corner (4:8–12). The high level of communalism that we see in the life of the Jerusalem church reflects an eschatological survival instinct (2:44–45; 4:32–37). The community experiences the same hostility from the 'kings of the earth' (Herod, Pontius Pilate) that Jesus suffered (4:23–31). The apostles rejoice that they have been 'counted worthy to suffer dishonour for the name' (5:41). Stephen explicitly identifies himself with the Son of Man who suffered and was vindicated. His last words echo Jesus' words from the cross (7:56–60). We should think of this as a quite deliberate and provocative imitation of Christ's martyrdom. It says to the leadership in Jerusalem: we are the community of the Son of Man, the righteous, who will receive the kingdom. Paul first encounters Jesus in the form of the persecuted, suffering community of the Way (9:4–5; cf. 22:6–11, 19; 26:9–15). Ananias is told that Paul is a 'chosen instrument of mine to carry my name before the Gentiles and kings and the children of Israel,' but what this means is explained in terms not of preaching the gospel but of suffering (9:15–16). As Christ suffered in Jerusalem, Paul will suffer in the diaspora world. Following his near fatal stoning in Lystra, he encourages the disciples, telling them that 'through many tribulations we must enter the kingdom of God' (14:22; cf. 20:23; 21:13). This is exactly the story of the Son of Man: the faithful community endures persecution from its enemies (an alliance of unbelieving Jews and idolatrous Gentiles: cf. Acts 14:5) until eventually régime change is brought about and the kingdom is given to the saints of the Most High.

The people of the one Creator God are under judgement, facing destruction. In a very concrete sense, through his death and resurrection Jesus has established the basis for a community that participates in the story of the Son of Man, through which that people will be saved. The announcement of this salvation in the Greek–Roman world is an announcement of the collapse, sooner or later, of an antipathetic pagan culture. But it also leads to the inclusion of Gentiles in a community that must still go through the storm of the wrath of God. That roughly is the story of the Gospels and Acts. In the next two chapters we will look at how that story plays out in the theological argument of Romans.

9

The Premise of the Promise in Paul's Argument in Romans

Paul's letter to the church in Rome starts with a brief exposition of the 'gospel of God' (Rom. 1:1–6). It is an announcement of 'good news' that was promised beforehand through the prophets – that is, it is consistent with an older sense of identity and purpose. It has to do with Jesus, a descendant of David according to the flesh, who was designated 'Son of God in power according to the Spirit of holiness by his resurrection from the dead.' Paul's responsibility as an apostle, as one who has been 'set apart' for this gospel, is to 'bring about the obedience of faith for the sake of his name among all the nations.' He then writes of his long-standing concern for the believers in Rome and of his eager wish to 'preach the gospel to you also,' because it is the 'power of God for salvation to everyone who believes, to the Jew first and also to the Greek' (1:15–16). This synopsis readily provides us with the basic components of Christian mission, conventionally understood: the preaching of the good news about Jesus with a view to the salvation of all people. But the conventional understanding misrepresents the narrative substructure that, for the most part covertly, has shaped Paul's thought. His elegantly tailored argument has been drastically cut up and restitched in order to suit a modern fashion.

In the first place, the gospel is an announcement about Jesus' status *with respect to Israel as a nation*. He is, or has become,

Israel's king, probably in the nuanced sense suggested by Psalm 2. Paul makes precisely this link in his sermon at Pisidian Antioch. The 'good news' that God raised Jesus is a fulfillment of the decree of the Lord in Psalm 2:7: 'You are my Son; today I have begotten you' (Acts 13:32–33). Jesus is the king of Israel who has been made God's son *today*. This 'today' draws our attention to the dramatic context in which the decree is made. The nations conspire against the Lord and his anointed king with the intention of breaking free from their bonds. God's response to this rebelliousness is to 'give birth' to the king as his 'son,' who will ask for and receive the nations as his heritage. The point of the metaphor is specifically the assurance that the king will overcome his enemies.

In this connection, secondly, it is instructive to read the phrase 'obedience of faith . . . among all the nations' against the background of Psalm 18:43–50, in which David celebrates the victory that the Lord gave him over his enemies: 'You delivered me from strife with the people; you made me the head of the nations; people whom I had not known served me. As soon as they heard of me they obeyed me; foreigners came cringing to me' (18:43–44). This gives a consistent narrative form: Jesus is the king who has been delivered from his enemies, and Paul has been called to the apostolic task of bringing about an obedient response from the nations – only it is an obedience characterized not by fear but by faith.

Paul will quote explicitly from this passage later in Romans with reference to the praise of the Gentiles: there will be praise among the nations because God has delivered Israel's king not only from his enemies (Ps. 18:48–49; cf. Rom. 15:8–9) but also from the 'cords of Sheol' and the 'snares of death' (Ps. 18:5). The argument here is very similar to that in Romans 1:1–6. The Gentiles will glorify God because of the mercy demonstrated in the story of Jesus (Rom. 15:8–9). Jesus becomes a 'servant to the circumcised to show God's truthfulness, in order to confirm the promises given to the patriarchs': he is the 'servant' who suffers and is killed for the sake of the future of the descendants of Abraham (cf. Isa. 52:13–53:12; Phil. 2:7). The quotation from Psalm 69:9 a little earlier in Paul's argument reinforces the point: 'Christ did not please himself, but as it is written, "The reproaches of those who reproached you fell on me" ' (Rom. 15:3). The psalmist, associating himself with the oppressed and needy in Israel, a people whom God has struck down in his wrath, suffers reproach from his enemies because 'zeal for your house has consumed me'; but he trusts that God will deliver him from his persecutors, and that in the end Zion and the cities of Judah will be rebuilt and reinhabited by 'those who love his name.' Paul superimposes this Old Testament drama of judgement, faithfulness and restoration on Jesus: he is redescribed as one who endured the sufferings of oppressed Israel because of the hope that God would remain true to his promise.

Thirdly, I will argue that when Paul insists that this 'gospel' about the deliverance of Israel's king from the enemies that conspire against him is the means of salvation for *all* who have faith (1:16), he is thinking in a rather specific and limited sense of the salvation of his contemporary world – the Jewish world first, but also the Greek–Roman world – from divine judgement. It is a mistake to read back into this argument our post-Enlightenment, universalizing perspective. We must stay within the narrative and see where it takes us.

Judgement on Israel

In the announcement about Jesus the 'righteousness of God is revealed from faith for faith' (1:17). There is the brief quotation from the prophet Habakkuk, to which we have already referred: 'The righteous shall live by faith' (Hab. 2:4). Then we have another explanatory statement: the righteousness of God is revealed because the 'wrath of God is revealed from heaven against all ungodliness and unrighteousness of men, who by their unrighteousness suppress the truth' (1:18). The connection between the *revelation* of the righteousness of God and the *revelation* of the wrath of God is emphatic: the one is in some sense a response to – an answer to – the other; and wedged tightly between them is Habakkuk's little aphorism about the righteous living by faith.

So in order to understand the 'gospel of God,' we must first consider what Paul meant by the 'wrath of God.' This is not a theme to which we instinctively warm – indeed, many would regard it frankly as barbaric. But we cannot make sense of the argument about faith, justification, and salvation in Romans without taking account of the fact that it is a response to the prospect of God's wrath against both the Jewish and the Greek–Roman worlds. The stress on impartiality at this point is important, but we should also take note of the fact that with respect to wrath the Jews in some manner *precede* the Gentiles (2:9–11). The immediate context offers no clue as to how this precedence is to be interpreted; the larger narrative, however, suggests that the judgement of God comes on Israel historically before it comes on the Greek–Roman world.

No doubt the phrase 'wrath of God' is meant to say something about God's attitude toward those who do not obey the truth, but it must be understood in the first place *objectively*, as signifying an event – a future 'day of wrath when God's righteous judgement will be revealed' (2:5), from which people will need to be 'saved' (5:9). In the Old Testament the 'wrath of God' is experienced as suffering and destruction, typically in the form of war. For example, if the people of Israel oppress the foreigners in their midst or maltreat any widow or fatherless child, God's wrath will burn: 'I will kill you with the sword, and your wives shall become widows and your children fatherless' (Exod. 22:21–24). In Zephaniah 1:15–16 the day of God's wrath against Jerusalem will be 'a day of distress and anguish, a day of ruin and devastation, a day of darkness and gloom, a day of clouds and thick darkness, a day of trumpet blast and battle cry against the fortified cities and against the lofty battlements.'

This is the conceptual background to Paul's argument. If Jesus could foresee a day of 'wrath against this people' when Jerusalem would be surrounded by armies, when its inhabitants would fall by the sword and be led into captivity, when the city would be trampled underfoot by Gentiles (Luke 21:20–24), there is no reason to think that Paul gave the term a quite different, unworldly, metaphysical spin. We do not have the same level of graphic detail in his letters, but even in Romans it is clear that the wrath of God against wrongdoing may be executed quite concretely and realistically by civil powers (Rom. 13:4). In 1 Thessalonians 2:16 he concludes his angry attack on the Jews who killed Jesus and obstruct the preaching of the gospel to the Gentiles with the vehement declaration that 'God's wrath has come upon them at last!' We cannot be certain what he had in mind, but it must have been an event or state of affairs within Israel's immediate historical experience – perhaps something of the nature of the expulsion of Jews from Rome by Claudius in AD 49 or the killing of ten thousand Jews during a riot in the temple in the same year (Suetonius, *Claud.* 25.4; Jos. *J.W.* 2.12.1; *Ant.* 20.5.3). Judgement would come as a day of 'tribulation and distress' (Rom. 2:9). The phrase in inverted form ('in your distress and in your tribulation') occurs three times in the Septuagint version of Deuteronomy 28:53–57 to describe the extreme suffering caused when the Lord brings an enemy to besiege the towns of Israel.

So the eschatological horizon of Paul's letter to the Romans is one of judgement, first on Israel, then on the Greek–Roman world. As in Habakkuk, the vision is hastening to its end. Paul expects his readers to have to face the day of wrath, but he is confident that they will be 'saved' from it – in fact the moment of their 'salvation' is fast approaching, the night is far gone, the day is at hand (Rom. 13:11–12; cf. 16:20). The same argument appears in 1 Thessalonians 1:9–10: the believers, who are imitators both of Paul and of the Lord because they 'received the word in much affliction,' who have become actors in the drama of the Son of Man, are waiting for Jesus from heaven, who will deliver them from the wrath to come (1 Thess. 1:6, 10).

A day of judgement, no different in *kind* to the Babylonian invasion centuries earlier, is rapidly approaching for Israel – an event that will have a catastrophic impact on the nation to which belonged 'the adoption, the glory, the covenants, the giving of the law, the worship, and the promises' (Rom. 9:4). The 'promises' include the promise to Abraham and his offspring that they would become a great nation that would inherit the world. So does the likelihood that hundreds of thousands of Jews will be killed or driven from the land and that the city of Zion, the place of God's presence, will be destroyed mean that the promise has failed (Rom. 9:6)? This, I think, is the central question that Paul addresses in Romans – indeed, it is the central question of the New Testament: How does God keep his promise to Abraham at this moment in history, as rumors of war begin to be heard? We are standing at the narrative intersection again: the story about judgement and suffering clashes with the story about a people called to be a world-within-a-world and threatens to terminate it.

The faithfulness of Jesus

The problem created by the law is that it has consigned a sinful Israel to inevitable destruction. If Israel had kept the law, the predicament would not have arisen; if the Jews had done what was good, there would have been 'glory and honor and peace' rather than 'tribulation and distress' (2:9–10). It is not the law that is at fault, but the people. Because, in Paul's argument, they have stolen, committed adultery, robbed temples, dishonored God, etc. (2:21–23), they cannot escape condemnation. The recalcitrant descendants of Abraham, the vehicle of the promise, are trapped in a system that is bound, sooner or later, to destroy them: the wages of sin is death, the consequence of rebellion is destruction (6:23). By appealing to the law, they merely confirm the judgement against them. The solution to the dilemma, therefore, must come *in a very practical sense* from outside the law.

It is important to keep in mind that as Paul sets off in this direction, he is pursuing an argument about Israel. The Jews have been granted certain benefits – notably they have been entrusted with the oracles of God (3:2). But when it comes to wickedness, they are no better off than the Greeks; they cannot expect preferential treatment; they are just as much under the power of sin as the rest of humankind. The Old Testament quotations strung together in Romans 3:10–18 all speak of corruption and injustice *within Israel* and the hope that God would act to punish the wicked and deliver the righteous 'poor' from their enemies.

The significance of the quotations is captured in the argument that follows. The law was given to Israel so that the all-pervasive power of injustice and corruption might be disclosed and the whole world held accountable to God (3:19–20). The law does not excuse Israel's sin, it does not justify: on the contrary, it is precisely because Israel is held accountable that the world is held accountable (cf. 3:6). Israel was meant to set the standard of righteousness. If it fell short of that standard, if it fell short of the glory of God, then the judgement prescribed by the law would come into effect – so that the whole world (Paul is thinking primarily of the Greek–Roman world) might be held accountable for its idolatry, immorality and injustice.

The righteousness of God revealed apart from the law

If Israel is to escape the coming destruction, therefore, it must be justified – in the law-court metaphor that organizes much of Paul's thought here – in some other way than by works of the law, because appeal to the law will only ever reinforce the guilty verdict. In Paul's mind, of course, there is an alternative to the law: Israel may appeal to the story about Jesus, which he restates metaphorically as an act of atonement (3:25). Here is the evidence that God is righteous, that he has not forgotten his promise to Abraham. In this story we find the manifestation of the righteousness of God 'apart from the law,' which is demonstrated in the 'faithfulness of Jesus Christ,'[1] whom 'God put forward as a *hilastērion* by his blood' (we have to insert the Greek word at this point because its translation is problematic).

The 'righteousness of God' in Paul's argument has to do fundamentally with *the integrity of God's commitment to his people*. The interpretive background is found in texts in the Old Testament that speak of God's righteousness as a response to the crisis of Israel's rebelliousness and humiliation. Isaiah 51:1–8 is especially important. God urges those in Israel who seek righteousness, the 'people in whose heart is my law,' to consider Abraham – the rock from which they were hewn, the quarry from which they were dug. They are reminded of the promise to bless him and multiply him. Zion will be comforted, her wilderness will be made like Eden, her desert like the garden of the Lord: Israel will be creation renewed. God's righteousness draws near: it will be demonstrated in the establishment of 'justice for a light to the peoples,' in the judgement of the nations that oppose Israel, and in the return of the 'ransomed of the Lord' to Zion (cf. Isa. 46:12–13; 51.11; 59:16–18). Paul speaks of an analogous ransoming or redemption, an analogous return from exile and renewal, that will show that God's commitment toward his people, which has its origins in the promise to Abraham, remains in force, despite the inescapable verdict of the law.

This is the announcement of 'good news' to Israel that was promised beforehand through the prophets. It is the announcement to Jerusalem and the cities of Judah that the Lord God is coming to restore his people; it is the announcement to Zion that 'Your God reigns,' that he will redeem devastated Jerusalem, that all the ends of the earth will see the salvation of Israel; it is the announcement to oppressed Israel that they will be set free from their captivity, that the ruined cities will be rebuilt, that they will be known by foreigners as 'priests of the LORD' (Isa. 40:9–11; 52:7–10; 61:1–6).

How, then, is the integrity of God's commitment to the descendants of Abraham demonstrated in the story about Jesus? When Paul spoke earlier in the letter of how the 'righteousness of God' was 'revealed from faith for faith,' he connected the thought with Habakkuk's saying about the righteous living by faith (Rom. 1:17). Habakkuk does not merely articulate some timeless spiritual principle here: his point is that when judgement comes on Israel in the form of conquest, the righteous person will live – that is, survive – by virtue of his faith or faithfulness or steadfastness (Hab. 2:4). We may suppose, therefore, that when Paul makes use of this saying in order to explain the revelation of the righteousness of God *at the present time* (cf. Rom. 3:26), he is thinking, in no less concrete terms, both of a destruction that will come upon Israel, and of an expression of faithfulness, trust, and steadfastness in the face of aggression. This is the story about Jesus, which, as will become clearer as we progress, has merely prefigured or pre-empted the suffering of the 'righteous' community that he called into being. His suffering and death are presented as an atoning sacrifice for the nation (3:25). He suffers the wrath of

God in the form of Roman execution, in anticipation of the judgement that will come on Israel, and is destroyed so that at least a remnant of Israel will not be destroyed. The community that is 'justified by his blood' will be saved from the coming wrath of God (5:9).

An atonement for Israel

In the Septuagint the word *hilastērion* mostly refers to the 'mercy seat' that covered the ark of the covenant (see Exod. 25:17–22). In Paul's argument the association with Christ's 'blood' or death suggests that the ritual on the Day of Atonement is in view: Aaron is instructed to take the blood of the 'goat of the sin offering that is for the people' and sprinkle it on and in front of the mercy seat; in this way he makes 'atonement for the Holy Place, because of the uncleannesses of the people of Israel and because of their transgressions, all their sins' (Lev. 16:15–16). Paul uses an idea, therefore, that is intimately associated with an act of atonement *for Israel's sins*. Jesus' faithful obedience culminating in his death at the hands of Israel's enemies was in some sense equivalent to, or analogous to, the action on the Day of Atonement by which Israel was cleansed of its sins.

So the righteousness of God with regard to the promise is established in Christ's death, which can be seen as an act of atonement not for every Tom, Dick or Harriet but for the nation. Paul's argument here is not that Jesus died for all humanity but that he died for Israel, and that Israel is therefore saved by his death from the wrath of God (Rom. 5:9). That is already the logic of the atonement theology, but it is a contentious claim and needs further support.

First, the forgiveness of Israel's sins and the restoration of the nation following the exile is sometimes presented in the Old Testament as an act of atonement. Isaiah 27:8–9 is a good example: God contended with the people by exile, but the guilt which brought this judgement upon them will be 'atoned for,' the sin of Jacob will be removed, when the people put an end to their idolatries. In order to redeem exiled Israel, God will give Egypt as an 'atonement' (Isa. 43:3: ESV has 'ransom'). Of particular interest is Daniel 9:24. The angel Gabriel explains to Daniel that the desolation of Jerusalem will last not seventy years, as he has read in Jeremiah (Dan. 9:2; cf. Jer. 25:11–12; 29:10); rather seventy weeks (of years) are decreed to 'finish the transgression, to put an end to sin, and to atone for iniquity, to bring in everlasting righteousness.' The restoration of Jerusalem following a protracted state of exile will be brought about by an atonement for the iniquity of the nation.

Secondly, Paul's use of the atonement metaphor is prefigured – as was Jesus' argument that his death would be a 'ransom' for many – in the extraordinary stories of the Maccabean martyrs: 'And through the blood of those devout ones and their death as an atoning sacrifice (*hilastēriou*), divine Providence preserved Israel that previously had been mistreated' (4 Macc. 17:22). The theology is straightforward: the wrath of God has come upon sinful Israel in the concrete form of the aggression of Antiochus Epiphanes; the hope of the martyrs is that their 'blood' will be the act of atonement by which this wrath will be brought to an end and Israel saved from destruction. This barely differs from Paul's argument in Romans: by his righteous death Jesus atones for the sin of Israel and brings to an end the wrath of God which is justly directed against the nation. At this point, however, the two arguments diverge significantly. The suffering of the Maccabean martyrs does no more than re-establish the *status ante*: the removal of the oppressor and the cleansing of Israel from Gentile influence. But the suffering of Jesus introduces something new – a transformation of the people that is epitomized by Jesus' resurrection as a new creation.

Thirdly, it is difficult not to hear echoes of the description of the suffering servant in Paul's argument in Romans 3 – 4. The servant suffers punishment (Isa. 53:5), however, not for the sake of the world but because Israel sinned: 'stricken for the transgression of my people' (53:8). This is not personal sin, it is not a universal atonement. It was the sin of the nation that brought the judgement of God upon it – exile, and the devastation of Jerusalem. At least, we must place the personal transgressions, the sins of individual Jews, within this larger story. In his suffering the servant experiences the judgement of

God against Israel; through his suffering many in Israel are accounted righteous; he bears their sins (53:10–12).

Justification of the ungodly by faith

Jesus' faithful obedience to the point of death on a Roman cross, therefore, marks out an alternative path to follow, an alternative way of being, for a people justified apart from the law. In this respect his death does for this people what the atonement sacrifice did for the nation: it provides *at the present time*, when God's patience is rapidly running out, an effective escape from the consequences of sinfulness; it provides salvation from the wrath of God.

But how exactly is this group of people 'justified?' They are justified at the intersection of the two stories about righteousness and faith. They are justified, in the first place, by demonstrating the sort of trust or faith in Jesus that Abraham originally displayed in the God who promised that he would be the father of a great nation. This is not faith in the abstract; at the heart of it, at least, is the specific conviction that God will fulfill this promise *under the present circumstances* even though the situation is apparently hopeless. The universalizing perspective, which expects to find in Romans an argument that transcends the contingencies of the narrative, can only hamper us here. We must read with the limited outlook of someone crossing the terrain at ground level, who cannot see beyond the next range of hills, beyond the immediate eschatological horizon.

This is where the second story, the eschatological subplot, comes into focus. Abraham's faith in the promise had to overcome the fact of his and Sarah's old age – and of course, later the command to sacrifice Isaac. Those who believe in Jesus, however, do so in defiance of the fact that they are a small, insignificant and unwelcome sect on the margins of Judaism, that they are bound to encounter distrust and sometimes outright hostility from their pagan neighbors, that the powerful and indeed satanic forces of Roman imperialism are drawn up against them and will sooner or later attempt to crush them.

They believe even though they have been told from the start that they can expect exactly the same treatment as Jesus received as the day of wrath, the 'last days,' approaches. *It is on account of this fundamental willingness to believe that God will not renege on his promise to Abraham and to trust the story about suffering and vindication, death and resurrection, that righteousness is counted to many* (Rom. 4:11–12, 22–24). This is the sort of faith – a steadfastness and loyalty – that will ensure that at the present time the 'righteous' will live. They cannot expect to escape suffering on the day of God's wrath, but they can expect not to be blotted out.

To be justified by faith is a narrative concept, not an abstract principle of salvation. The 'righteousness' or 'rightness' of those who believe the promise has to do with something to come in the future – the vindication of the suffering community (represented by the Son of Man motif) and the establishment of the renewed people of God in the world under Christ as king. The essential character of faith in Romans is certainly not propositional belief. It is also more than a private reliance on God to intervene and fix things. It is the sustained trust of the community in the God who vouchsafes the future of the descendants of Abraham.

It is not the law that will ensure the survival of the people of God in the world, it is faith or faithfulness: faith in the God who promised to Abraham that his descendants would inherit the world, faith in the God who would not let the 'righteous' be destroyed on the day of wrath. This is the basis for the sense of 'peace with God' that Paul speaks of in Romans 5:1 – it is the concrete assurance that the coming disorder and destruction is no longer directed against them. The believers stand in a place of grace: they are where Christ was when he faced the prospect of suffering, when he faced his accusers, when he was reviled and beaten, and in the end crucified by the instrument of God's wrath against Israel. So Paul can affirm that they rejoice in their sufferings knowing that suffering produces endurance, and endurance produces character, and character produces a hope that will not put them to shame – a hope of sharing the glory of God (5:2–5).

10

The Night is Far Gone but it is Illumined with Nero's Torches

Israel faced destruction because, for all its privileges, it could not escape the inexorable law of sin and death that had been in force since Adam. But just as all humanity, Jew and Greek alike, found itself implicated in Adam's sin, so a new humanity would be implicated in Jesus' act of righteousness (Rom. 5:15–21). Despite its many trespasses (5:16), renewed Israel would experience the life of the age to come.

The manner in which the 'many' participate in the life of the one man Jesus Christ is set out in Romans 6. The important point to grasp is that Paul does not put forward the death and resurrection of Christ simply as a metaphor for the conversion of the believer. What he describes, at some level at least, is a much more realistic fellowship in Jesus' suffering and vindication. To have been baptized into his death, to have been united with him in the likeness of his death, for the old self to have been crucified with him, is to anticipate the suffering of the community. The sinful nature that rebels against God is put to death so that the believer may walk in newness of life; but to walk in newness of life is to anticipate – either directly or through the collective experience of the community – a sharing in the likeness of Jesus' resurrection.

Conformed to the image of the Son

This thought is developed further in Romans 8. Those who are 'in Christ Jesus' are no longer condemned by the law of sin and death, they are no longer subject to wrath; they have been set free to *live* according to the Spirit. They are under obligation, therefore, to 'put to death the deeds of the body' – in the language of Ephesians and Colossians, to put off the old humanity (cf. Eph. 4:22; Col. 3:9). Their spirits are alive because they have the 'spirit of Christ': they are walking the same path, with the same purpose, with the same faithful obedience, with the same spirit. Because they have the spirit of the one who suffered and was vindicated, they have no need to fear suffering (Rom. 8:15). Like Jesus they are 'sons of God.' If they are children, then they are also heirs of God, inheritors of the promise. But there is a further possibility: they may also be fellow heirs with Christ *if* they suffer with him in order that they may also be glorified with him (8:17).

The 'if' is crucial. A person who has been set free from the law of sin and death by the Spirit is an heir of God and will inherit the promise to Abraham: he or she will become part of the renewed people of God. This is the first narrative about a recreated microcosm in the midst of the nations and cultures of the world. Those who *suffer*, however, in the way that Christ suffered, have a rather different prospect: they will be glorified as Christ was glorified. This is the second narrative about the vindication of the Son of Man, and it becomes the theme of the second part of the chapter.

The 'sufferings of this present time' that Paul speaks about in Romans 8:18 are not the ordinary, or even the extraordinary, aches and pains of life – sickness, unemployment, bereavement, conflict, and so on. He is not saying that life sucks but everything will be wonderful when we get to heaven. What he has in mind is a quite specific and limited historical circumstance – the suffering of the community *with Christ* in this 'present time' of eschatological crisis, the union with him in the likeness of his death. Its nature is made clear in verse 35: it is the experience of tribulation, distress, persecution, famine, nakedness, peril, the sword. These are the sufferings of a community that remains faithful to the calling to proclaim the good news that God has saved his people through the death and resurrection of Jesus, as the day of wrath approaches. They recall Paul's accounts of the hardships he himself endured for the sake of Christ: danger, hunger, and nakedness are listed in 2 Corinthians 11:23–27; distress and persecutions in 2 Corinthians 12:10. Perhaps more significantly, Jesus had warned his 'brothers' (Paul will pick up on this 'relationship' in Rom. 8:29) that they would suffer hunger, thirst, nakedness, sickness, imprisonment, and the neglect and contempt of the unrighteous (Matt. 25:31–46).

The experience is summed up in the words of Psalm 44: 'For your sake we are being killed all the day long; we are regarded as sheep to be slaughtered' (Rom. 8:36). The Psalm speaks of military defeat and the scattering of the people of Israel among the nations to become the 'taunt of our neighbors, the derision and scorn of those around us . . . a byword among the nations, a laughingstock among the peoples' (Ps. 44:13–14). This is a *Christ-like* experience, and it is what Paul is talking about when he speaks of being 'conformed to the image of his Son' (Rom. 8:29). Again this must be understood in a quite specific sense: it is the image of one who suffered and was glorified, who died and was raised from the dead. Those who are conformed to the image are those who share the experience. In this way Christ will be the 'firstborn among many brothers': he was the first to suffer and be raised from the dead (cf. Col. 1:18; Rev. 1:5), but he will not be the only one. Nothing will separate the suffering community from the love of the God who raised Jesus as firstborn from the dead. Just as the Maccabean martyrs 'conquered' the tyrant Antiochus through their endurance (4 Macc. 1:11), they are 'more than conquerors' (Rom. 8:37).

It is worth reminding ourselves at this point that seven or eight years later the church in Rome was subjected to intense and inhuman persecution. By AD 64 the Christian community had become sufficiently separate from Judaism, sufficiently influential, and sufficiently distrusted to be made scapegoats for a fire that destroyed two-thirds of the city. This is what they had to overcome. Tacitus regarded the sect as a 'most mischievous superstition,' but he was clearly taken aback by the extreme cruelty of their suffering:

Accordingly, an arrest was first made of all who pleaded guilty; then, upon their information, an immense multitude was convicted, not so much of the crime of firing the city, as of hatred against mankind. Mockery of every sort was added to their deaths. Covered with the skins of beasts, they were torn by dogs and perished, or were nailed to crosses, or were doomed to the flames and burnt, to serve as a nightly illumination, when daylight had expired. Nero offered his gardens for the spectacle, and was exhibiting a show in the circus, while he mingled with the people in the dress of a charioteer or stood aloft on a car. Hence, even for criminals who deserved extreme and exemplary punishment, there arose a feeling of compassion; for it was not, as it seemed, for the public good, but to glut one man's cruelty, that they were being destroyed. (Tacitus, *Annals* 15.44)

The eager longing of creation

But how does the argument about creation (Rom. 8:19–23) fit into this? In a rather remarkable way, Paul transcribes the story of the suffering community onto creation. Creation has been 'subjected to futility,' is in 'bondage to decay,' has been 'groaning together in the pains of childbirth until now,' and is impatient for the 'revealing of the sons of God'; creation itself will 'obtain the freedom of the glory of the children of God.'

The background to this idea is found in Isaiah's vision of an earth corrupted by the sin of its inhabitants. Because the people have 'transgressed the laws, violated the statutes, broken the everlasting covenant,' the earth mourns and withers, is defiled, is devoured by a curse (Isa. 24:4–6; cf. 7:23–25; Jer. 4:27–28; 12:4, 11). It is part of God's judgement on the world that the earth will be made desolate and plundered (Isa. 24:1, 3). The imagery is brutal: 'The earth is utterly broken, the earth is split apart, the earth is violently shaken. The earth staggers like a drunken man; it sways like a hut; its transgression lies heavy upon it, and it falls, and will not rise again' (Isa. 24:19–20). Behind this, no doubt, is the original story of the cursing of the ground because of Adam's disobedience (Gen. 3:17–18), but the overarching narrative of judgement and restoration that emerges in Isaiah is more important for understanding Paul's argument. If the corruption of the earth is a consequence of the sin of its inhabitants, the restoration of God's people will be accompanied by a renewal of creation. When Israel is led out of captivity and exile, the mountains and hills will break into singing, the trees will clap their hands, the cypress will grow in the place of the thorn, the myrtle will replace the brier (Isa. 55:12–13). It will be as though God has created 'new heavens and a new earth' (Isa. 65:17). The story of Israel's sin will be forgotten.

We return to Paul's argument. The sufferings of God's people are an effect of eschatological transition, they are the 'sufferings of this present time,' a by-product of the wrath of God that is coming upon the world; so it is appropriate that creation is implicated in this. But the suffering will culminate in glory, and poetically Paul imagines the created order eagerly waiting to see the moment when the sons of God will be revealed, when their tormented bodies are redeemed. Creation is portrayed *as a spectator* in the drama of the Son of Man. But what are we to suppose happens to creation itself?

It is usually assumed that the revelation of the sons of God and the liberation of creation belong to the same eschatological moment, but this is not necessarily the case. The fact that Paul thinks of creation waiting eagerly not for its own liberation but for the revelation of the sons of God suggests that he regards the redemption of the bodies of those who suffer (at the *parousia*, at the vindication of the Son of Man) *as an anticipation* of the final liberation of creation from bondage to decay. Creation looks forward to seeing the vindication of the suffering and faithful church because in that revelation of glory it will glimpse something of its own ultimate transformation. The story of creation and the story of vindication intersect: the glory that will be given to the Son of Man community when its enemies are overcome, when the pagan world is judged, prefigures the eventual glory that creation itself will receive when all things are renewed and death has been destroyed.

The body of Christ

Chapter 8 ends with Paul's confident assertion that the suffering community of Christ's 'brothers' will be 'more than conquerors' in this present time of eschatological crisis; they will be conformed to the image of the Son who was called to suffer, was vindicated or 'justified,' and was glorified. In chapters 9 to 11 we have a lengthy and somewhat parenthetic discussion of the implications both theologically for the promise to Abraham and on a more personal level for Paul's own kinsmen as the day of wrath approaches.

The prospect of war and enormous suffering explains the 'great sorrow and unceasing anguish' that Paul feels on account of his brethren (Rom. 9:2–3): they are 'vessels of wrath prepared for destruction' (9:22). It is the same anguish that Jesus experienced as he approached Jerusalem and wept over it because the people had missed the opportunity for peace – not a vague inner sense of being right with God but peace that is an absence of war: 'the days will come upon you, when your enemies will set up a barricade around you and surround you and hem you in on every side and tear you down to the ground, you and your children within you' (Luke 19:43–44). Paul later quotes a text about a 'stone of stumbling, and a rock of offence' that is laid in Zion (Rom. 9:32–33). It comes from a passage in Isaiah that records a 'decree of destruction from the Lord GOD of hosts against the whole land,' addressed to the 'scoffers, who rule this people in Jerusalem.' Because of their dishonesty and corruption, they will not escape death when the 'overwhelming scourge' passes through the city (Isa. 28:14–22). It is in direct response to this prospect of destruction, perhaps especially of Jerusalem, that Paul expresses his heart's desire and prayer to God for them that they may be saved (Rom. 10:1). The salvation of Israel that he speaks about at length and with a patent sense of urgency in these chapters must be understood in simple historical terms: it is not a widespread conversion of Jews to Christ for which we are still waiting today; it is the avoidance of a devastating war with Rome. We know the outcome. Israel persisted in its unbelief. War was not avoided. Only a few were saved.

Then Paul introduces the final section of the letter with an appeal to the 'brothers' in Rome to 'present your bodies as a living sacrifice, holy and acceptable to God, which is your spiritual worship' (12:1). What I think he does here, though we do not have space to develop the argument, is resume in a rather deliberate manner the theme from Romans 8 of the community that is called in imitation of Christ and for the sake of the promise to Abraham *to suffer sacrificially out of obedience to God*. The verse is a call to suffer faithfully, perhaps picking up the allusion to the offering of Isaac in Romans 8:32: present your bodies as Isaac's body was presented as a 'living sacrifice,' even though the prospect of death would appear to jeopardize the promise to Abraham that his descendants would be a new creation. It then provides the framework for the practical teaching that follows. So it is specifically the *suffering* community that is 'one body in Christ' – they follow the narrow path of suffering not as isolated individuals but corporately, serving one another. They are to love one another with 'brotherly' affection. They are exhorted to a zeal, fervor, patience, and constancy that will keep them faithful in the face of tribulation. Significantly, they are to bless those who persecute them, they are not to retaliate against their enemies or seek revenge, because the day of God's wrath is coming. The night is far gone; deliverance from suffering is close at hand.

The connection between the body metaphor and the theme of suffering is less apparent in 1 Corinthians, but even here the community that is one body in Christ is the community which must survive the day of God's wrath (1 Cor. 3:13), which will 'inherit the kingdom of God' (6:9), which will have to endure the 'present distress' and the passing away of the form of this world (7:26, 31), and which at the end of the ages faces intense pressure to revert to the worship of idols (10:6–14). And notice where Paul's description of the interdependence of the parts leaves us: if one member of the body *suffers*, the whole body *suffers*; if one member is 'glorified,' all rejoice together (12:26). 'Glorified' may be an overtranslation of *doxazetai* here: most English versions would have something like 'honored.' But we have seen in Romans 8 that those who *suffer* with Christ are *glorified* with Christ, that God *glorifies* those who are conformed to the image of the Son who *suffers* and is vindicated (8:17, 30). It is at least arguable that integral to the condition of being the body of Christ is the shared experience of suffering and of the 'glory' that attaches to those who remain faithful *in extremis*. It is as a 'body' that the brotherhood of the Son of Man suffers with Christ and is glorified with Christ.

The worship of the nations

The people that will survive the day of wrath will consist not only of Jews but also of Gentiles (Rom. 9:22–24). This is an immediate consequence of the fact that righteousness has been established *apart from the law*, to be pursued instead by faith or by faithfulness (9:30–31). We have the same argument in Ephesians 2:11–22. Gentiles participate in the commonwealth of Israel because Jesus' death *for the sake of Israel* had the effect of abolishing the law which divided Jews and Gentiles. Jesus died directly for Israel, but *indirectly* for the Gentiles. This was an unexpected development for those Jews who believed themselves to be renewed Israel in Christ; but Paul argues that it is clearly foreseen in the Old Testament. Christ became a servant to the circumcised for two reasons: first, to confirm the promise to Abraham that his descendants would 'inherit the world'; secondly, in order that the 'Gentiles might glorify God for his mercy' (15:8–9). Here we have the missiological paradigm, with its origins in Isaiah, that we encountered in the Gospels and in Acts: God saves Israel through the faithfulness of Jesus, and this salvation elicits both admiration and participation from the Gentiles.

The string of quotations that follows is again highly instructive:

> As it is written, 'Therefore I will praise you among the Gentiles, and sing to your name.' And again it is said, 'Rejoice, O Gentiles, with his people.' And again, 'Praise the Lord, all you Gentiles, and let all the peoples extol him.' And again Isaiah says, 'The root of Jesse will come, even he who arises to rule the Gentiles; in him will the Gentiles hope.' (Rom. 15:9–12)

David will praise God among the nations because he has delivered him from his enemies (Ps. 18:46–49). In the Septuagint translation of Deuteronomy 32:43 Moses exhorts the nations to rejoice with Israel because God will avenge the blood of his people and bring judgement upon his enemies. The brief Psalm 117 urges the nations to praise the Lord because of his steadfast love toward his people. Lastly Paul quotes verbatim from the Septuagint version of Isaiah 11:10: 'the root of Jesse will come, even he who arises to rule the Gentiles; in him will the Gentiles hope.' This verse belongs to a prophecy about a descendant of David who will rule the land with righteousness, upholding the cause of the poor and defeating the wicked: creation will be renewed because knowledge of the Lord will fill the whole land; the 'banished of Israel' will be gathered from their places of exile among the nations; and their enemies will be defeated.

It is because Israel has been delivered from its enemies and restored as a new creation following judgement – that is, because God has shown mercy to his people – that the nations will praise God. Paul's task, as he understands it, is to make this 'praise' of the Gentiles a concrete, community-based reality across the Greek–Roman world: he is a 'minister of Christ Jesus to the Gentiles in the priestly service of the gospel of God, so that the offering of the Gentiles may be acceptable, sanctified by the Holy Spirit' (Rom. 15:16). This is all part of the eschatological 'moment,' an event in the dramatic transition from second-temple Judaism to the age of a global people, taught by the Spirit, consisting not only of Jews but also of Gentiles, dispersed throughout the world as a new creation. Paul orchestrates the response of the nations as part of the climax to the story of Israel's redemption, and then we move into something else.

Judgement on the Greek–Roman world

The wrath of God comes first on the Jewish world, then on the Greek–Roman world. Let's go back to Habakkuk. If the Chaldeans were to be the means by which God would punish Israel for its wickedness, they themselves would nevertheless not escape punishment: 'Woe to him who makes his neighbors drink – you pour out your wrath and make them drunk, in order to gaze at their nakedness! You will have your fill of shame instead of glory. Drink, yourself, and show your uncircumcision! The cup in the LORD's right hand will come around to you, and utter shame will come upon your glory!' (Hab. 2:15–16; cf. Isa. 51:22–23; Jer. 25:15–29; Lam. 4:21). They would drink from the same cup of wrath that they forced upon Israel. Just as he waited for God to judge the wicked in Israel, Habakkuk will 'quietly wait for the day of trouble to come upon people who invade us' (Hab. 3:16).

In the same way, in Paul's argument, wrath on Israel will be followed by wrath on the Greek–Roman world – again, I would suggest *specifically* on the Greek–Roman world. This is a broad inference partly from the distinctive forms of pagan idolatry, immorality, and injustice that are held up for condemnation, and partly from the eschatological narrative and the sense of immediacy that we encounter in Romans 13:11–12. At the close of the letter Paul assures a community that will soon have to bear the brunt of Nero's ingenious savagery that the 'God of peace will soon crush Satan under your feet' (Rom. 16:20). This is not an indefinite or abstract hope. He means that God will defeat the satanically inspired opposition of Roman imperialism. Babylon the Great will fall. Then there will be heard the loud voice of a great multitude in heaven: 'Hallelujah! Salvation and glory and power belong to our God, for his judgements are true and just; for he has judged the great prostitute who corrupted the earth with her immorality, and has avenged on her the blood of his servants' (Rev. 19:1–2). This is the victory that will finally ensure the continuation of the promise to Abraham.

The two quotations about righteousness and faith and their associated stories that lie at the heart of Romans provide answers to two questions. The first is: Who are the true descendants of Abraham? The second: How will God keep his promise to Abraham when Israel according to the flesh is a herd of panicked pigs running headlong toward a precipice? The answer to the second question is 'through the faithfulness of Jesus,' which gives us the clue to how the first question must be answered. But lurking behind these *who* and *how* questions is a *why*. Why does it all matter? Why is God so concerned about the descendants of Abraham, whoever they might be, however they might be saved from destruction? As we have seen, righteousness is attained through faithfulness, but this righteousness or justification is not an end in itself.

Imagine that a doctor is sued for malpractice. After a lengthy, exhausting, and bitterly contested trial he is acquitted: he has been put in the right before the law, he has been justified or vindicated, and the threat of disqualification or imprisonment has been removed. While it lasts, the trial is all-consuming; but it is not the whole story of the doctor's life. The doctor has been saved from punishment by the verdict, but he has also been saved to continue his career: his vocation to heal has been validated, confirmed. The trial is merely a difficult and painful episode in the larger narrative.

Paul's letter to the Romans represents the arguments put forward at Israel's trial for malpractice. The difference, of course, is that Israel was in fact guilty and, as we shall see, the 'career' could be saved only by going outside the law. But the analogy remains valid. The drawn-out legal proceedings are merely an episode in a larger story about the descendants of Abraham, and we are occasionally reminded of the original vocation: he is to be the father of a numerous people, of many nations, who will inherit the world (4:13, 17). We are slowly making our way back to this.

11

The Coming of the Reign of God in (what was) the Foreseeable Future

The story so far. Israel was conceived at the outset as a reinstatement of creation following the repeated failure, at both the individual and the societal level, of the original project. Israel would be a world-within-a-world, characterized as such by the four spheres of its existence. The first three spheres define a self-contained creation in microcosm: worship of the living God in the midst of things; an internal commitment to social righteousness and justice; and a productive and responsible relationship to its physical world as a species that exercises dominion in the image of the creative God (cf. Gen. 1:26–27). The fourth sphere of its existence has to do with the 'within-a-world' aspect of this microcosm. Israel had to coexist with other peoples and cultures. The possibility that this coexistence would lead to the extension of the original blessing to the nations never fully receded, but proximity generated tensions that in the end proved highly destructive. One crucial consequence of the fact that Israel continually rubbed up against the surrounding nations was that it came to think of itself increasingly in 'national' terms as a people governed by a king who would go out and fight against its enemies. So 'kingdom' became the controlling template for the creational microcosm.

It came to pass, of course, that the microcosm fell apart with the exile to Babylon, because Israel did not observe the statutes and commandments that should have regulated its internal life, leading to the loss of the original blessing and defeat by its powerful neighbors. It is a basic premise of the New Testament that this state of defeat persisted, in effect, right down to the dramatic appearance of John the Baptist in the wilderness announcing that the kingdom of God was at hand. It is important to note that this premise is *politically* defined – in the sense that it has to do with the collective behavior and destiny of a people. The 'gospel' is an announcement about what God has done for his people; it is not put forward merely as the solution to a problem of universal sinfulness.

In simple terms Jesus performed two roles. First, *as a prophet to Israel* he confronted the nation with a stark choice: it could stay on a political-religious course that within a generation would lead to war and appalling destruction; or it could find an alternative path of repentance that would lead to survival and the life of the age to come. Secondly, *as the Christ* he self-consciously took upon himself the identity of the Son of Man of Daniel's vision, in two respects. On the one hand, he acted out in advance and alone the story of a community that must suffer at the hands of Israel's enemies, be raised from the dead, and eventually be given sovereignty and kingdom by the Ancient of Days. On the other, he gathered around himself the nucleus of that community, preparing them through teaching and example to walk this same path of suffering, resurrection, vindication, and kingdom for the sake of the future of the people of God, for the sake of the defining promise to Abraham. This is the very practical sense in which as Israel's 'king' he *saved the nation from its enemies.*

Over the next three decades we see small, insecure, and sometimes unstable fellowships of the Son of Man come into existence across the Greek–Roman world. They are the fruit of the announcement of good news that is made throughout the domain of Israel's enemies, which is that God is acting to bring judgement to an end and to deliver his people from oppression. This is the means by which the promise to Abraham of creational blessing will be salvaged – the means by which God will demonstrate his righteousness.

These scattered communities exist in defiance of the controlling hierarchies of the Greek–Roman world. They refuse to participate in the customary pagan immoralities, they refuse to give the time of day to the hollow gods of the various local and imperial pantheons, they refuse to accept the displacement of the Creator by the god Caesar. Just as Jesus defeated the principalities and powers on the cross (cf. Col. 2:15), so the early church believes that through its faithful suffering it will overcome the idolatrous, unjust, life-distorting hegemony of imperial Rome. Their defiance, of course, gets them into trouble. The 'mission' of the church within the outlook of the New Testament is to challenge the political and religious hubris of Rome, the arch-enemy of YHWH – and then to survive the backlash that such a challenge will inevitably provoke. But they have faith in the God who overturns the tables of history and makes all things new.

Coming soon . . .

We cannot escape from the sense of an impending and decisive change in the scheme of things that runs through the writings of the New Testament, much as different writings today – books, magazines, newspapers, blogs – may be pervaded with premonitions of environmental disaster. We are in the habit of overlooking these really quite unambiguous statements, perhaps with the excuse that not even Jesus knew the day or the hour, or that 'with the Lord one day is as a thousand years, and a thousand years as one day' (2 Pet. 3:8). But this misses the point. The New Testament affirms the *nearness* of a dramatic and far-reaching turn of events not out of unbridled apocalyptic enthusiasm but because these fledgling communities of Christ faced a level of hostility that conceivably would crush the movement and bring the promise to nothing. It is not a matter of getting the timing right. It is a matter of how long the early church will have to wait before the suffering comes to an end. Peter recognizes that scoffers will ask, 'Where is the promise of his coming?', but he insists that 'the Lord knows how to rescue the godly from trials, and to keep the unrighteous under punishment until the day of judgement' (2 Pet. 2:9; 3:3–4).

Paul gives instructions about marriage in 1 Corinthians 7 that take into account the 'present distress,' but he reassures the church that 'the appointed time has grown very short . . . the present form of this world is passing away' (1 Cor. 7:29, 31). He urges the believers in Rome to 'be patient in tribulation,' to bless those who persecute them, but assures them that 'salvation is nearer to us now than when we first believed. The night is far gone; the day is at hand' (Rom. 12:12, 14; 13:11–12). The God of peace will *soon* crush their opponent under their feet (Rom. 16:20). The Thessalonians suffer affliction, but they will be delivered from their enemies at the *parousia* of the Lord, which he expects to happen within his lifetime (1 Thess. 3:4; 4:15–18; cf. 2 Thess. 1:4–10; 1 Cor. 15:51–52). The Ephesians are instructed to put on the 'whole amour of God' so that they may be able to 'withstand in the evil day' (Eph. 6:13). This 'evil day' is not the absolute end of history; it is a 'day of the Lord' – the chaos and destruction through which the judgement of God is expressed, when the Lord protects the righteous from their enemies (cf. in LXX Ps. 41:1; 48:6; Prov. 16:2, 9; 24:10; 25:19; Jer. 17:17–18; Amos 5:18–20; 6:3). The point is that Paul believes that the church in Ephesus faces such a day. It is not a speculative possibility; it is not a tenet of faith, inserted somewhere near the bottom just after the line about the body of Christ and the true universal church. It is something that will happen to the believers in Ephesus *within a foreseeable future*, and it is of the utmost importance that they know how to stand firm. The writer to the Hebrews addresses a community that is slipping backwards alarmingly under persecution and encourages them to stand fast, to keep meeting, 'all the more as you see the Day drawing near' (Heb. 10:24–25). James urges the 'twelve tribes in the Dispersion,' whose faith is being tested through 'trials of various kinds,' to be patient 'until the coming of the Lord . . . for the coming of the Lord is at hand' (Jas. 1:1–2; 5:7–8). Likewise, Peter informs the 'elect exiles of the dispersion' (1 Pet. 1:1), who suffer in the flesh as Christ suffered, who suffer in a way that is replicated by their 'brotherhood throughout the world,' that the 'end of all things is at hand' (1 Pet. 4:1, 7; 5:9; cf. Rom. 8:29). This is the brotherhood of the Son of Man (although it sounds too much like a 1970s pop group) waiting for vindication and an end to their afflictions.

The collapse of classical paganism

In the broadest terms the coming 'Day of the Lord' is thought of as an act of divine judgement on the entire pagan world. Paul has the audacity to announce in the middle of the Areopagus in Athens that God will no longer overlook the wrong-headedness of a culture that conceives of the divine being as an object of 'gold or silver or stone, an image formed by the art and imagination of man.' They should abandon these beliefs and their associated practices because the whole edifice of classical paganism is about to collapse: God 'has fixed a day on which he will judge the world in righteousness by a man whom he has appointed' (Acts 17:29–31; cf. 10:42).

His argument in Romans is sharper. The wrath of God will come upon Israel first, but it will also come upon the Greek–Roman world because the repudiation of the 'immortal God' in favor of 'images resembling mortal man and birds and animals and creeping things' has resulted in characteristic forms of 'unrighteousness': the 'dishonoring of their bodies among themselves' and a whole catalogue of social evils (Rom. 1:18–31). We do not have space here to discuss the details of Paul's analysis of the spiritual and moral corruption of pagan society – certainly not to defend or excuse his views on homosexuality. But we can put forward the general argument that he is not speaking about a universal and final judgement on all humanity. What he has in mind essentially is a historically limited judgement that will come upon the Greek–Roman world because of its characteristic idolatry, the unrighteousness that ensues from it, and its entrenched antipathy toward the God of Abraham.

Undoubtedly there is a universal premise behind this argument going back to Adam: all people have sinned, have fallen short of the glory of God, and so deserve death (cf. Rom. 3:23; 5:12). But the 'day of wrath' constitutes a particular historical outworking of the general principle with reference not primarily to individuals but to nations or cultures – a moment in history when 'God's righteous judgement' is revealed (2:5). Sudden destruction, Paul warns in his letter to the church in Thessalonica, will come upon a world that says, 'There is peace and security' (1 Thess. 5:3). This is not a generic characterization of human society: it is a quite pointed allusion to the ideology of Roman imperialism that guaranteed *pax et securitas*. We can hardly escape the conclusion that Paul thought of this 'Day of the Lord' specifically as a day of judgement on the hubris and idolatry of Rome.

The defeat of YHWH's enemies

Just as YHWH is imagined in the Old Testament descending with the hosts of heaven to defeat Israel's enemies, so in the prophetic mind of the early church the hope emerges that the Lord Jesus will 'descend' to defeat those who are persecuting them. David, for example, his life threatened by his enemies, called upon the Lord: 'Bow your heavens . . . and come down! Touch the mountains so that they smoke! Flash forth the lightning and scatter them; send out your arrows and rout them! Stretch out your hand from on high; rescue me and deliver me from the many waters, from the hand of foreigners' (Ps. 144:5–7). The New Testament vision is no more literal and no less realistic than this. When Paul tells the Thessalonians that at the *parousia* the 'Lord himself will descend from heaven with a cry of command, with the voice of an archangel, and with the sound of the trumpet of God' (1 Thess. 4:16), he constructs from the language of Old Testament prophecy a symbolic narrative about the preservation of the whole people of God at a time of eschatological crisis. It will be the deliverance from the 'wrath to come' for which the Thessalonian believers, who 'received the word in much affliction,' who have renounced their idols, wait (1 Thess. 1:6, 9–10).

In the heightened apocalypticism of 2 Thessalonians – remember, we are still down the rabbit hole, in a strange and sometimes surreal world – antagonism toward the church is concentrated in the figure of a 'man of lawlessness . . . who opposes and exalts himself against every so-called god or object of worship, so that he takes his seat in the temple of God, proclaiming himself to be God' (2 Thess. 2:3–4). This is a notoriously difficult passage to interpret, and I can only summarize here the argument that is worked out in *The Coming of the Son of Man.*[1]

The story that Paul tells as a response to the Thessalonians' experience of persecution is essentially a reworking of the events surrounding the political and religious crisis provoked by Antiochus Epiphanes that is 'foretold' by Daniel. In Daniel's narrative a blasphemous and overweening king attacks Jerusalem, desecrates the temple, and takes away the 'regular burnt offering,' exalting himself above every god and speaking 'astonishing things against the God of gods' (Dan. 11:31, 36). Many Jews are seduced by the king and forsake the covenant, but the wise, the people who know their God, stand firm: they help others to understand, 'they shall stumble by sword and flame, by captivity and plunder,' but through their suffering they are 'refined, purified, and made white, until the time of the end' (11:32–35). The affliction of that time will be more severe than anything that the nation has previously experienced. But eventually the king will be defeated militarily, and the people 'shall be delivered, everyone whose name shall be found written in the book.' Many who have died will be raised – some to 'everlasting contempt' but many to 'everlasting life.' These are the Jews who stood firm against Antiochus' aggressive campaign of Hellenization: 'those who are wise shall shine like the brightness of the sky above; and those who turn many to righteousness, like the stars for ever and ever' (11:45 – 12:3).

This story is transposed, either by Paul or more likely by an interpretive tradition that goes back to Jesus, into a contemporary key in order to give narrative shape to the new conviction that God will ultimately rescue and vindicate the beleaguered community. Paul's man of lawlessness, who 'opposes and exalts himself against every so-called god or object of worship, so that he takes his seat in the temple of God, proclaiming himself to be God,' is an opponent *like Antiochus* – Nero would be an obvious fulfillment of the type, but it does not need to be limited to him. The 'rebellion' or 'apostasy' that must come first is a shorthand reference to the corruption of Jewish religious life that gives him the opportunity to sabotage the covenant and desecrate the temple. What restrains the slide into lawlessness for a while at least is the activity of the wise, who give understanding to many, who lead many to righteousness. But in the end the supreme adversary of the brotherhood will be revealed, 'whom the Lord Jesus will kill with the breath of his mouth and bring to nothing by the appearance of his coming' (2 Thess. 2:8). This is the moment of the *parousia*, when the enemies of the church will be defeated and punished: they will have no part in the age that will follow the collapse of Roman imperialism, they will be excluded from the 'presence of the Lord.' Then the Son of Man community will have rest from its afflictions, and it will receive the kingdom for which it has been qualified by its sufferings (2 Thess. 1:4–9).

The resurrection of the dead in Christ

The *parousia* of the Lord will be accompanied by the resurrection of those who died 'in Christ,' who therefore have participated quite realistically and concretely in the story of the Son of Man. Just as Jesus died and rose again, so those who imitated him in his suffering and death would rise again in order to share in the vindication of the faithful church. This is the argument that Paul puts to the Thessalonians, who are troubled by the fact that some of their number have already died.

We are accustomed to thinking that resurrection in the New Testament occurs in two stages: Jesus' resurrection in the middle of history and a final resurrection at the end of history. I think this schema needs to be adjusted. The basic distinction to be made is between, on the one hand, a resurrection in connection with the restoration of the people of God following a period of extended judgement and, on the other, a resurrection of *all the dead* prior to a final judgement and renewal of creation. We have seen already how closely the hope of resurrection is associated in the Old Testament with the rescue of oppressed Israel and in the Maccabean literature with the belief that YHWH would ultimately vindicate the martyrs who suffered for the sake of the traditions of the fathers. This provides us with the primary template for understanding resurrection in the New Testament: it reflects the hope that God will remain true to his promise to Abraham and raise oppressed Israel to new life, both metaphorically and literally. The significance of *Jesus'* resurrection for his followers is that it anticipates this limited corporate hope and gives them reason to think that God will deliver them from death in the same way. So the resurrection of the 'dead in Christ' at the *parousia* constitutes the fulfillment of the primary template (1 Thess. 4:16). It is not to be equated with the final resurrection of all the dead: rather it marks a climactic moment in the story of the Son of Man, which is the story of the deliverance and restoration of God's people.

Paul's compressed apocalyptic schedule in 1 Corinthians 15:20–28 can be read in the same way. He speaks of Christ being raised in advance of the resurrection of the dead 'who belong to Christ' – as the 'firstfruits of those who have fallen asleep' (1 Cor. 15:20–23). The 'end' comes some time later, once all his enemies have been defeated, including death itself, and the kingdom is given back to God the Father. We can superimpose on this the closing symbolic narrative of the book of Revelation. Following the defeat of Babylon the Great, which is Rome, the satanic power which inspired it is imprisoned in the pit, and those who lost their lives because of 'the testimony of Jesus and for the word of God' are brought back to life and reign with Christ for a thousand years. This is explicitly labeled the 'first resurrection' (Rev. 20:4–6). At the end of the thousand years, following a final skirmish with Satan, a 'great white throne' appears, all the dead are raised and 'judged by what was written in the books, according to what they had done' (20:11–13). Those whose names are not written in the book of life are thrown into the lake of fire, which is the second death, along with Death and Hades. Now we have come to the final and absolute defeat of all Christ's enemies and the renewal of all things: 'Then I saw a new heaven and a new earth, for the first heaven and the first earth had passed away, and the sea was no more' (Rev. 21:1).

From the perspective of the New Testament communities, however, this is an utterly remote prospect. What concerns them as a matter of intense personal and communal hope is the 'first resurrection,' which is the outcome of God's commitment to his suffering people during a time of crisis. As Paul tells the story in 1 Thessalonians, at the *parousia* both the living and the dead will be united with the Lord as he comes on the clouds of heaven to bring to a conclusion the drama of the Son of Man. In this way the Son of Man is both Jesus and the community that has suffered in him. In this way the community shares in his vindication and receives 'dominion and glory and a kingdom.'

The mind of Christ . . .

At this point, at the conclusion of the interim story about the Son of Man, we are in a position to say quite clearly what the 'Kingdom of God' is. First, we may say that the *coming* of the kingdom of God constitutes the climax of the long narrative of Israel in its struggle to recover spiritual integrity and independence from an oppressive overlord. It means that God has come to forgive and reform his people, to judge the culture that threatened to obliterate it, and establish his own reign through a proxy in the place of the hierarchies of political and spiritual powers that opposed him. This is what the disciples were asking for when they prayed, 'Your kingdom come.' The kingdom of God is not conceived as being in principle or even *potentially* a reign over all the peoples of the earth: it is a reign over the family of Abraham in the midst of the peoples of the earth.

This is consistent with the Old Testament hope, which is not the globalizing one that all the nations will become subject to YHWH but that *YHWH will reign over Israel in a globally significant way*. When God comes to reign over his people, the event will have a far-reaching impact on the nations; they may even in some way come to participate in the event; but the ambition is only that Israel will be God's people in the midst of other nations and cultures.

The argument of Psalm 2, for example, is not that the Lord's anointed will come to reign over the nations but that when the kings of the earth violently oppose the God of Israel and his people, they will inevitably be defeated – broken in pieces like a potter's vessel. The same circumstances are envisaged in Psalm 110: the enemies of Israel's anointed ruler will be defeated on the 'day of his wrath,' when God will 'execute judgement among the nations' (Ps. 110:5–6). These are critical texts for the New Testament understanding of the role played by the Christ in the restoration of Israel; they have distinctive interpretive significance and should not be unthinkingly assimilated into a later normalized 'Christian' perspective.

Psalm 96 has the marvelous acclamation, 'Say among the nations, "The LORD reigns!" ' But the confession is grounded in the expectation of an imminent act of judgement on behalf of Israel. The earth rejoices because he 'comes to judge the earth. He will judge the world in righteousness, and the peoples in his faithfulness' (96:10–13). The narrative aspect of the theological statement is underlined by the fact that the Psalm forms part of David's hymn of praise on the day when the ark is brought back to Jerusalem (1 Chr. 16:8–36). It celebrates the faithfulness of God who remembers his covenant with Israel, and concludes with a prayer for deliverance: 'Save us, O God of our salvation, and gather and deliver us from among the nations, that we may give thanks to your holy name, and glory in your praise' (16:35). Similarly Psalm 97: the Lord reigns because he has established righteousness and justice by defeating the enemies of Israel. It is a demonstration of the fact that he is 'exalted far above all gods'; those who worship images are put to shame. But in the end he is still the God who 'preserves the lives of his saints; he delivers them from the hand of the wicked' (Ps. 97:10).

Secondly, 'kingdom' has been taken away from the vaunting oppressor and given instead to the Son of Man, the representative and embodiment of righteous Israel, the servant who suffered because of the sins of the nation. The story is told powerfully and emblematically in Paul's account of Christ's journey of suffering and exaltation in Philippians 2:6–11. The difficult statement about Christ not counting 'equality with God a thing to be grasped' makes best sense when seen as expressing an ambition antithetical to the type of the blasphemous king who aspires to divine status. In Daniel's narrative this is the 'little horn' on the head of the fourth beast, the king who will 'speak words against the Most High,' who will 'exalt himself and magnify himself above every god, and shall speak astonishing things against the God of gods' (Dan. 7:25; 11:36). Paul invokes the type in his description of the 'man of lawlessness' who 'opposes and exalts himself against every so-called god or object of worship, so that he takes his seat in the temple of God, proclaiming himself to be God' (2 Thess. 2:4). So the argument in Philippians 2:6 is that Christ did not seek to plunder or seize by force the status of being equal with God in the way that Caesar had as the embodiment of the type of the man of lawlessness. He is the *anti-Caesar* who wins the battle between the microcosm and the macrocosm through an absolute faithfulness to the one Creator God.

Because of his obedience in suffering, Christ is exalted by God and given the 'name that is above every name' so that at the name of Jesus 'every knee should bow, in heaven and on earth and under the earth, and every tongue confess that Jesus Christ is Lord' (Phil. 2:9–10). This last part is an allusion to a passage in Isaiah that affirms resoundingly both that YHWH is the only Creator God (Isa. 45:18) and that it is YHWH alone who will defeat Babylon, bring back the 'remnant of the house of Israel,' the 'survivors of the nations,' and restore Zion (Isa. 45:20; 46:3, 13). The vigorous polemic that runs through this passage is directed not against the Gentiles but against those scattered, exiled Jews who were inclined to believe that the gods of Babylon – Bel and Nebo – were more powerful than the God of Israel. The one, therefore, to whom 'every knee shall bow, every tongue shall swear allegiance' (Isa. 45:23) is the one who will save Israel from the ends of the earth. So the implicit argument in Philippians 2:6–11 is that Jesus is the one who through his suffering would bring to an end Israel's extended captivity, the continuing state of judgement, who would overcome the Babylon-like oppressor, and who would receive from his people the worship that would otherwise be given to the gods of the nations, supreme among them Caesar himself.

The story is told, however, for the sake of the integrity of a community that must make the same eschatological journey: 'For it has been granted to you that for the sake of Christ you should not only believe in him but also suffer for his sake, engaged in the same conflict that you saw I had and now hear that I still have' (Phil. 1:29–30). They will be saved from the hostility of their opponents by being *Christ-like* – by being united in love, by looking after the interests of others, by having among themselves the mind of Christ, who made himself nothing, a servant, who suffered, was put to death by the enemies of YHWH, but who was raised and given the name which is above every name. Or as Paul argues in Romans, they are conformed to the image of the Son who suffered and was glorified, so that he becomes the 'firstborn among many brothers'; they endure until the day of salvation by putting on the Lord Jesus Christ (Rom. 8:29; 13:14). This is the sense in which they will work out their salvation with 'fear and trembling' (Phil. 2:12): they will act in a way that will ensure that they do not disintegrate as a believing community under persecution. They are called to shine as lights in the midst of the 'crooked and twisted generation' of the contemporary Greek–Roman world, holding fast to the word of life – the promise that the descendants of Abraham will survive the wrath of God that is coming on the ancient world – so that 'in the day of Christ I may be proud that I did not run in vain or labor in vain' (2:12–16).

Paul's emphasis on having the mind of Christ reminds us that for all the apocalyptic fireworks of a passage like 2 Thessalonians 2:8–12, the vindication of the suffering church will be achieved not least through righteous behavior. The same point comes across very clearly in 1 Peter: 'Keep your conduct among the Gentiles honorable, so that when they speak against you as evildoers, they may see your good deeds and glorify God on the day of visitation' (2:12). The 'good deeds' are not optional extras – they are an intrinsic part of the 'defense' on the day of God's judgement against the ancient world. In *The Rise of Christianity* Rodney Stark makes the sociological observation that one of the main reasons Christianity won out over Greek–Roman paganism was the compelling power of an exceptional, self-sacrificing ethic – the 'good deeds,' for example, of the Christians who refused to abandon plague victims.[2] This was a precise fulfillment of Peter's prediction. Paganism was completely wrong-footed by the compassion and courage of this Christ-like people.

From our perspective, therefore, the coming of the kingdom is no longer the proper ultimate hope of the church. The reign of God that is foreseen in the New Testament finds its narrative fulfillment in the victory of the early church over Rome. The prophetic projectile, constructed from material mined in the Old Testament, that was launched at the outset of Jesus' short-lived career, has finally reached its target. What it means to us now is that *Christ is Lord:* he reigns at the right hand of God with those who died and were raised with him; and because Christ now reigns over the restored microcosm, *the missional orientation shifts from establishing the kingdom to being a renewed creation,* just as we shift from a story about conflict with the nations and the vindication of the faithful community to a primal story about a people called to model for the world an authentic humanity. By the time we get to the appearance of a new heaven and new earth in Revelation 21, 'kingdom' language has dropped out of the narrative – as Paul expresses it in 1 Corinthians 15:24, at the end there are no more enemies and the exercise of 'kingdom' becomes irrelevant; it is handed back to God the Father.

12

It's a Small World After All . . .

Jesus' eschatological horizon – in effect, the outer boundary of his future – was the war against Rome, the destruction of Jerusalem and the temple, and the vindication of the community of his disciples for having left the broad road and taken the difficult and painful Way that would lead to life. The eschatological horizon of the emerging churches, however, even in the years before AD 70, was split. There was the same belief that Israel faced national disaster and that if the heirs to the promise to Abraham were to survive, they would have to undergo a fundamental redefinition. This is evident from Peter's speeches in the early part of Acts and from Paul's argument in Romans 9 – 11. But these communities escaped from the frying pan of God's judgement on Israel only to land in the fire of conflict with Greek–Roman paganism and the arch-adversary of the people of God. So a second eschatological horizon comes into view – the extended historical 'moment' when this opposition is overcome, persecution is ended, and judgement is given in favor of the seminal community, this time for having stood firm against a profoundly idolatrous worldview and the corruption of creation that stemmed from it.

The two horizons are linked by a narrative formula supplied by the Old Testament: God judges his rebellious people by means of a powerful enemy, a remnant is saved, and the enemy is itself defeated. Within this narrative, mission consists in the prophetic proclamation of judgement and hope, the gathering of a renewed community that eventually, and almost incidentally, includes Gentiles, the announcement to the nations that YHWH has redeemed his people through the faithfulness of the Christ, and the active resistance of the church to paganism in order to ensure that ultimately Christ and not Caesar will reign over God's new creation.

By this point we appear pretty much to have exhausted the teaching of the New Testament about the future mission of the church, which leaves us in a bit of a quandary. How are we to define a continuing purpose *in the aftermath* of this protracted eschatological crisis – that is, in historical terms and with hindsight, after the disintegration of national Israel, the eventual legalization of Christianity, the sacking of Rome by the Visigoths, and the demise of classical paganism?

The New Testament and post-eschatology

First, I would argue that the New Testament is not unaware of the fact that the church would not merely continue to exist but would fulfill its purpose beyond the second horizon of judgement on the Greek–Roman world. Paul, for example, speaks of a 'day' that will 'disclose' the quality of the work done by those building on the foundation of Jesus Christ. He is not talking about a final judgement – the 'Day of the Lord' is never a *final* judgement in Scripture, and the final judgement is not a 'day of the Lord.' What he has in mind is a period of opposition and persecution – probably the period of 'distress' to which he refers in 1 Corinthians 7:26 – that will severely test the faith and faithfulness of the community. Anything constructed from flammable materials such as wood, hay, and straw will be burnt up in this eschatological 'fire.' Only those parts built from gold, silver and precious stones will escape being reduced to ashes. But the point of the metaphor is that it is the task of the apostles and others to *build a church that will still be standing after the crisis of the end of the age*, and it is on that basis that they will be judged and rewarded. If the community is spiritually immature, riven by jealousy and rivalry, arrogant, disputatious, complacent about idolatry and immorality, the chances are that many of them will give up when the going gets tough. This is why Paul is so anxious that they should grasp the significance of the message about 'Christ crucified,' why he wants them to have the 'mind of Christ,' and why he insists that this community of the Son of Man must be founded on Christ. These are eschatological concerns. Without that specific foundation, without the deeply instilled character of the Son of Man, the church may find itself burnt up in the fires to come – and then there will be no *post-eschatological* church, only charred remains smoldering in some neglected backstreet of the pagan world.

If, as I argued earlier, a significant period of time is expected to intervene between the resurrection of those who died in Christ at the *parousia* and the 'end,' when the kingdom is restored to the Father (1 Cor. 15:23–24), then we have a place in Paul's schema for the post-eschatological church. But a much clearer case can be made from the final chapters of Revelation. Between the 'first resurrection' of the martyrs following the defeat of Rome and the final resurrection of all the dead we have a symbolic period of a thousand years, during which the martyrs reign with Christ in heaven and Satan is enchained in the bottomless pit (Rev. 20:1–6). The interim story of the Son of Man has come to an end: the dark forces of opposition have been judged and destroyed, the saints of the Most High have been raised and vindicated. But the church goes on. We are told nothing at this point about the nature of its existence, but it is there amidst the nations and cultures of the earth, so that when Satan is released at the end of the thousand-year period, he deceives the nations of the earth again and leads them to launch an attack on the 'camp of the saints and the beloved city' (20:9).

If we can shade our eyes from the glare of John's apocalypticism, I think that we may discern here a realistic vision of the place of the church in the world, according to which it owes its freedom from the extreme, all-encompassing, and ultimately satanic hostility of pagan culture to the faithful suffering of countless small fellowships of the Son of Man. But it does not tell us much more than that. So how do we construct a 'mission' for the church in this indefinite, post-eschatological 'millennial' period? We do so, I think, in the first place, by recovering a creational and creative vision – both by looking back to the original vocation of the people of God and by embracing with John the final and genuinely transcendent prospect of a new heaven and a new earth. In other words, we return at last to the other story of faith and righteousness: we are *in the right place* with God when we believe or trust that he will preserve a people for his own possession, who are called to be a microcosm of the original creation.

New creation in Christ

There is nothing in the New Testament to suggest that the original calling of Abraham to be the progenitor of a new humanity, a creational microcosm, a world-within-a-world, has been abrogated or superseded in Christ. On the contrary, Paul's argument both in Romans and Galatians is precisely that Christ is the means by which God remains faithful to his promise to Abraham when the vehicle of that promise is about to career wildly into the brick wall of Roman exasperation and be written off. Christ died for the sake of the microcosm. So we need to bring to the surface the creational language in the New Testament that has been submerged beneath the dominant eschatological narrative.

First, the main story that is told about the Christ in the New Testament is the story about suffering, death, resurrection, and kingdom – in other words, the story of the Son of Man. But at a number of points a prior *creational* role is attributed to him, as the one through whom all things were created (e.g. John 1:1–3, 10; Col. 1:15–16; Heb. 1:2; 2:10). The effect of these statements is to superimpose the dimensions and dynamics of the original creation on the existence of the community that has its origins in Christ. It is first the community of the Son of Man; but beyond the eschatological crisis and the vindication of the suffering church the people of God becomes again a creational microcosm *under the form of the Christ through whom all things were made*. The form of Christ modulates as we switch narratives following the *parousia* – from the Son of Man through whom Israel is restored to the creational Word through whom the microcosm is re-established and sustained. I think that we can see in this switch a critical narrative-historical transition in the early understanding of the Christ: the firstborn from the dead necessarily comes to be understood as the firstborn of a renewed creation.

The one through whom the world was made becomes the source of life and light for those who believe in him: as a result they are born again, so to speak, as a creation-shaped community, 'born, not of blood nor of the will of the flesh nor of the will of man, but of God' (John 1:13). It is a community that must *suffer* first: the life of the age to come will be attained by participating in the story of the Son of Man who must be lifted up (John 3:14). But through the story about the Son of Man the promise given to Jacob as he slept outside the city of Luz is recovered (John 1:51).

The point is made in compressed form in 1 Corinthians 8:6: 'one Lord, Jesus Christ, through whom are all things and through whom we exist.' The 'we' of the church draws its identity from the creational Christ. In Colossians 1:15–20 this simple formula acquires poetic elaboration. The one who is 'firstborn of all creation,' through whom and for whom all things were created, who holds all things together, has become the beginning of a new humanity in which the full scope of the microcosm is repaired and reconciled to the Creator God. The phrase 'firstborn from the dead' reminds us that this is first a community that must suffer and be raised. Christ owes his pre-eminence in this new world to the fact that he was the first to walk the difficult path of suffering and death (Col. 1:18). But for the creational potential of this renewed people to be realized we must look beyond the story about suffering and vindication and ask what it means to be in Christ not only as the one who died and rose again (the story of the Son of Man) but as the one who embraces in himself the full purpose and integrity of creation.

Secondly, a person who has been baptized into Christ is described by Paul as having put off the old humanity and having put on the new (Eph. 4:22–24; cf. Col. 3:9–10). The transformation is conceived quite overtly as a renewal of creation. She is instructed to 'put off' the old person, the former self, which is 'corrupt through deceitful desires' – the corruption that the created order suffers because of human wickedness and idolatry (cf. Gen. 6:11–12; Isa. 24:23–25; Rom. 8:21). She is 'renewed' in the spirit of her mind, and then puts on the new self or person, '*created* after the likeness of God in true righteousness and holiness' (Eph. 4:24). In Colossians 3:10–11 this is a 'new self, which is being renewed in knowledge after the image of its creator,' part of a new humanity, chosen by God as Abraham was chosen (cf. Isa. 41:8), in which 'there is not Greek and Jew, circumcised and uncircumcised, barbarian, Scythian, slave, free.' The corruption of the old order has been overcome. Through Christ's death 'one new man' was created (Eph. 2:15). If anyone is in Christ, 'he is a new creation. The old has passed away; behold, the new has come' (2 Cor. 5:17).

Thirdly, the hope of the early church was in the broadest sense one of vindication: the concrete expectation, first, that the community of Jesus' disciples would be saved from the wrath of God and established as the authentic descendants of Abraham; and secondly, that Christ and not Caesar would become the definitive image of deity. For many this vindication would be a matter of 'going to heaven.' Those who died for the sake of the gospel, for the sake of the future of the people of God, for the sake of the promise to Abraham, would not go unrewarded. They would be raised and seated with Christ at the right hand of the Father. For the church it meant an end to oppression and the calling to be a redeemed humanity defined not by law and nationhood but by the Spirit and by reconciliation across the fissures of race, class, and gender. But the horizon of the *post-eschatological* church – that is, *our* horizon – is given to us at the end of Revelation. John sees 'a new heaven and a new earth, for the first heaven and the first earth had passed away, and the sea was no more' (Rev. 21:1). The new Jerusalem descends from heaven and finds its place in the midst of this new creation so that it can now be said, 'Behold, the dwelling place of God is with man. He will dwell with them, and they will be his people, and God himself will be with them as their God' (21:3). This is something quite different from the old creation. Death and Hades have been destroyed in the lake of fire (20:14); there shall be no more mourning or crying or pain (21:4); the human wickedness that vitiated the old creation has been eradicated (21:8).

Whereas in Daniel's judgement scene a river of fire issued from the throne of the Ancient of Days (Dan. 7:10–11 LXX), in the new creation it is the 'river of the water of life' that flows from the throne of God and of the Lamb (Rev. 22:1). This is also the river that 'flowed out of Eden to water the garden' (Gen. 2:10) and the river that flows from beneath the threshold of the restored temple in Ezekiel 47:1–12. Once again we find ourselves shifting symbolically between the two narrative archetypes. In the story of the Son of Man the oppressor of righteous Israel is destroyed in the river of fire; but in Ezekiel's vision the river that flows from the presence of the living God sustains life: 'on the banks, on both sides of the river, there will grow all kinds of trees for food. Their leaves will not wither, nor their fruit fail, but they will bear fresh fruit every month, because the water for them flows from the sanctuary. Their fruit will be for food, and their leaves for healing' (Ezek. 47:12). In John's sublime reworking of this image, the 'leaves of the tree were for the healing of the nations' (Rev. 22:2).

This is an ultimate hope, but it should exert a backward pressure on the self-understanding of the church. Even under the difficult conditions of the redemptive story about the kingdom of God we have seen how the creational motif lies not far beneath the surface. With sovereignty having been transferred to the Son of Man, who is the Christ through whom all things were made and remade, the *post-eschatological* church is in a position to reinterpret its calling in the light of the final hope. We endeavor to anticipate, prefigure, rehearse the new creation that rises like a full moon through the clouds, above our indefinite horizon. Arguably, this is what Christendom did in its heavy-handed way, for better or for worse. It constructed the microcosm, according to the paradigms of human society that were immediately to hand, as a highly organized, hierarchically governed polity with the aim of bringing the whole world under its intellectual, cultural, religious, and sometimes political sway. Now, as the church emerges from the model, methods, and mindset of Christendom, it must *re-form* itself and find new *postmodern* ways to bring the microcosm to life and recapture the original blessing.

The mission of the post-biblical church

The route that we have taken in the direction of a biblical theology of mission has made it difficult to generate much in the way of practical advice. On the one hand, I have argued unhelpfully that very little of the New Testament directly addresses the condition and calling of the post-eschatological church – which means we are also, therefore, a *post-biblical* church. We are off the map. If this is the case, we must seize the positive option, which is that it is precisely our calling, as those who have put on the Christ through whom all things were made, that we use our imaginations to create and recreate the microcosm, always as both reality and sign, as both life and art. On the other hand, this has been primarily an exercise in storytelling, and stories resist the powerful forces of systematization and utility. The story is not a tree to be cut down and sawn up into generalized principles and practices: it is a living thing to be climbed in, sat under, and wondered at. It is simply a story, and a story simply needs to be told and retold. Having said that, however, it is probably worth drafting some of the headings under which this telling of the story encourages us to speak about mission.

Crisis? Which crisis?

I would suggest that mission has too often been undertaken on the assumption that we face the same eschatological conditions – and the same *eschatological crisis* – as the New Testament. The whole world is under judgement because of sin, so the argument goes, and needs to be saved by the death of Christ so that people may know God in this life and be certain of gaining eternal life after death. It has been the missional responsibility of the church – of the evangelical church, at least – to ensure that as many people as possible are given the opportunity to hear this 'good news.' My argument is that this way of thinking about mission only really makes sense within the limited historical perspective of the New Testament: Israel is under judgement because of its habitual rebellion against YHWH; the promise to Abraham is rescued by the faithfulness of Jesus, who gave himself as an atonement for Israel's sin, so that the people might survive the wrath of God and have the life of the age which has now come; the salvation of Israel also means hope for Gentiles when time is running out for classical pagan culture; and finally, those who suffer with Christ are given the same hope of resurrection and exaltation to the right hand of God in heaven.

In this book I have taken what is perhaps a disproportionate amount of space to retell this intervening story of salvation because it is important to understand how it must be contextualized historically and bracketed narratively. But the struggle to survive the eschatological crisis was for the sake of what we now should understand as the mission or calling of the church, which must be redescribed in terms of the first story, as God's response to a *creational crisis*, the widespread failure of the macrocosm. That response, I would argue, is not fundamentally to redeem the world, or repair it: that is not the biblical missional paradigm. It is, in the simplest terms, to be an alternative humanity in the midst of things.

An authentic humanity

If the church has come into existence as the recovery of the promise to Abraham, then we should think of it as being, either actually or prophetically, *creational* in scope: it is a continuation of the microcosm that became Israel, albeit under rather different terms and conditions. The church should understand itself in the first place, therefore, as a *people*, an expansive expression of human community. It retains the sense of being one family, having Abraham as a symbolic ancestor. The ingrained divisions of a humanity at odds with itself, exacerbated by misunderstanding, greed, and a propensity toward violence, have been transcended. The boundaries between nations and cultures and the barriers that cut across nations and cultures have no validity in the small world that has inherited the calling of Abraham to experience the original creational blessing: 'There is neither Jew nor Greek, there is neither slave nor free, there is neither male nor female, for you are all one in Christ Jesus. And if you are Christ's, then you are Abraham's offspring, heirs according to promise' (Gal. 3:28–29).

As descendants of Abraham the church is *created* before it is saved. The story of the microcosm is not, in the first place, one of God saving fallen creation but of God bringing into existence a new creation. This prioritization factors down in principle to the individual. There is always going to be a sense in which people are *saved* from something as they come to participate in the microcosm – from a personal state of sin or futility or crisis. We become part of a process of renewal that will culminate in the final re-creation that is described in Revelation 21 – 22. But the narrative still suggests that post-eschatological 'evangelism' should be essentially an invitation to participate in the new creation project under the story of the Son of Man.

In accordance with the creational directive to be fruitful and multiply and fill the earth, the symbolic descendants of Abraham are a dispersed people. They represent – in a way that geographically challenged Israel could not – the claim of YHWH to be Creator of the whole world. For that reason a renewed humanity is bound to manifest itself in diverse forms. It shares in and is always to some extent subject to the complexity and multifariousness of the macrocosm. So it is probably better to say that the church exists as multiple prophetic experiments in the reinstatement of creation, all of them wrapped up in different ways in the possibilities that are found in their environment, all of them having the potential to capture the distinctive being of an authentic humanity, all of them telling the story, more or less coherently, more or less honestly. It is like a child blowing bubbles, each one a self-contained world, each one reflecting in its bright surface the beauty and pain of the macrocosm. The story looks something like Figure 12.1.

At every level of fragmentation and contextualization, however, the creational paradigm remains intact – just like fractals, the same pattern is revealed at all levels of magnification. Ideally at least, in even the smallest iterations we see, both actually and prophetically, the living God present through the Holy Spirit, the concrete outworking of compassion

macrocosm

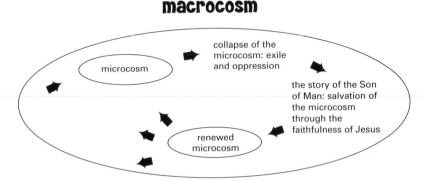

Figure 12.1 The story of authentic humanity

and justice, respect and thankfulness for the natural environment, a passion for creativity in the image of the creative God, and an acute sense of having to exist exposed, vulnerable, and visible in the midst of the nations and cultures of the world. Every community of believers is a sign of the whole people of God, a sign of renewed humanity, a sign of the goodness of the Creator, a sign of righteousness, a sign of the sheer profligate inventiveness of the Spirit.

The space, lastly, in which these creational values are put into practice is not the cramped little bed-sit of the individual life but the rambling mansion of the community. Holiness and righteousness are community values, not private virtues. They take the form of justice and compassion. The post-eschatological church cannot express a preference for the metaphysical over the material, the spiritual over the ethical, the mystical over the political, the private over the public. Its calling is precisely to integrate these polarities in concrete expressions of human community and through that to demonstrate the plausibility of righteousness in the world.

The outer space

The new creation in Christ is no longer *in competition with* the nations and cultures of the world, because the totalizing, satanically inspired ideology that would set up humankind in the place of God has been defeated: the beast has been destroyed, Satan has been chained and shut up in the abyss, the kingdom has been given to the Son of Man. The point here, of course, is not that these forms of idolatry and aggression are never seen again but that they no longer have political authority over the people of God, they can no longer threaten to annul the creational promise to Abraham. Because Christ and those in him overcame death, the church can be a channel of the original blessing to the world – not least because it may provide an unassailable alternative to ideological tyranny in whatever form it manifests itself. In its ambition to embody and advocate the fundamental goodness of God's creation the church is bound to be – if only incidentally – a resistance movement against prevailing patterns of idolatry and the corruption of personhood and community that stems from it.

Although this takes us into rather abstract territory, I think that just as Israel was understood as God's own people in the midst of the nations of the earth, the church must be alert to what is happening at the interface between the microcosm and the macrocosm. If the church is blessed, it will be a blessing. If it captures something of an authentic existence, it will find inevitably that it exists *for the sake of others*; and this 'for the sake of others' creates a significant missional hinterland, outside the church, in an outer space. The emerging post-Christendom church does not aspire to control, which is why it appears at times so hesitant to make absolute truth claims. It is only a red balloon floating in the middle of the room. But it may aspire to generate around itself a sphere of influence and credibility, where it is encountered and trusted as a priestly community for others. That is the purpose of our Soul Parties in The Hague: they offer as a gift community and meaning that stem from the renewal of creation. Projects such as Serve the City offer as a gift distinctive forms of hope that have their origins in the original blessing of humanity. This is not *instead of* being God-centered. It is *because of* being God-centered.

What we discover in ourselves as we struggle under grace to give substance and visibility to the hope of new creation, we *give to others* – knowledge of God in our midst, a practiced righteousness that transcends the instincts of greed and self-preservation, a commitment to relationships that resists the corrosiveness of contemporary culture, a deep experience of the goodness and beauty of the created world, an imaginative life inspired by the Spirit of the creative God; and because we never forget the other story about suffering and redemption, a love that is prepared to die so that others may live. We give these things away because we have too much of them. We have experienced something of the original blessing of the world, and we give it to others.

A storytelling community

I have added the qualification at a number of points that the church is new creation *both actually and prophetically*. To some extent the church must concretely *be* – must *struggle* to be – an authentic humanity according to the biblical pattern: that is, to repeat, a creative people centered on the living God, manifesting communal righteousness, and respectful of the material environment. It is a presumptuous ambition that can be realized only in the tension between obedience and grace. But out of this very imperfect and partial *being*, the people of God become a *sign* of the real thing. So the challenge facing the post-Christendom church is to re-imagine what it means to be a prophetic community – a community that by telling its story in the world, not just verbally or artistically but through the various practical elements of its shared life, narrates an alternative mode of being human. When Mosaic in Glasgow joins up with the Friends of the River Kelvin to restore a small sliver of the natural world as part of their worship, they are doing some good; but more importantly, they are acting out a story about the God who made all things good and who desires again to walk with us in the garden.

In this prophetic calling I think we find some necessary escape from the pretension and anxiety of being better than others. If we are not ourselves kings and queens, heroes and adventurers, we are nevertheless actors who delight in playing the parts. So what if we can do no more than rehearse the renewal of creation in a rather shabby, stumbling fashion, without the costumes and make-up and the lights, unsure where to stand, with lines poorly memorized? So what if the only place to rehearse our story is at the margins of society, on the fringes of our culture? At least the story gets told – that this is not our world, it is God's; he desires justice and mercy; he has brought a new creation people into existence and demonstrated to them that he is consistent and faithful and believable; there is something profoundly *right* about being human in this way.

The mission of the church is to be a creational microcosm, a creative community, a people committed to the volatile, adventurous task of always extracting the best from the world that God has brought into existence. But we do so without ever forgetting to tell the other story of the long exodus made by the early church, in Christ, through a wilderness of suffering and testing toward vindication. If the Lord's Prayer was a prayer to be spoken by the eschatological community, then we repeat it now as an act of remembrance. If the domestic ritual of the Lord's Supper was an act of association with the Son of Man who suffered for the sake of the future of the people of God, then we repeat it now as an act of remembrance, as an act of communal storytelling: this is our history, this is what we are thankful for, this is what has made us who we are, and we can never escape from it. The story about an authentic humanity, with its origins in the calling of Abraham to be blessed and be a blessing, continues to be told – indeed, lived out – because at a crucial juncture it intersected with a story about the Christ who died and rose again and who incorporated in himself a seminal fellowship in his sufferings that would overcome both Jewish and pagan hostility. This is the heart of Jesus' vision: the angels of God ascending and descending on the Son of Man.

For further information and discussion of the material in this book visit www.opensourcetheology.net/remission.

Notes

1. Re: Re: Mission

[1] www.glasgowmosaic.com.

[2] www.thewell.be.

[3] www.soulparty.org.

[4] In the context of this discussion 'eschatology' refers to a set of ideas or beliefs about the theological significance of decisive future events. The term 'apocalyptic' refers to the distinctive form of discourse that these ideas and beliefs may take in the Bible and related literature.

[5] Perriman, A. C., *The Coming of the Son of Man: New Testament Eschatology for an Emerging Church*, Milton Keynes and Waynesboro, GA: Paternoster, 2005.

2. Two Bedtime Stories and a Preview of Paul's Argument in Romans

[1] Cf. ESV: 'And on the wing of abominations shall come one who makes desolate, until the decreed end is poured out on the desolator.' The Greek translation of the Old Testament known as the Septuagint (LXX) is occasionally cited where there is a significant difference in text or meaning.

5. The Difficult Road Leading to Destruction

[1] Borg, M. J. and Crossan, J. D., *The Last Week*, New York: HarperCollins, 2006, 2–3.

9. **The Premise of the Promise in Paul's Argument in Romans**

[1] The meaning of the phrase *dia pisteōs Iēsou Christou* is, of course, much debated. My basic argument would be that the translation 'through the faithfulness of Jesus Christ' makes much better sense within the eschatological narrative that I think underlies Paul's thought in Romans than the more traditional rendering 'through faith in Jesus Christ.'

11. **The Coming of the Reign of God in (what was) the Forseeable Future**

[1] Perriman, *The Coming of the Son of Man*, 130–152, 157–164.
[2] Stark, R., *The Rise of Christianity*, New York: HarperCollins, 1997 (first published 1996), 83–88.

Atonement for a 'Sinless' Society
Engaging with an emerging culture

Atonement for a 'Sinless' Society

Engaging with an Emerging Culture

Alan Mann

'Sin doesn't really exist as a serious idea in modern life,' wrote the journalist Bryan Appleyard. He is not alone in his views. 'Sin' has become just as tainted, polluted and defiled in the postmodern mind as the word itself indicates.

Atonement for a 'Sinless' Society is about an encounter between two stories: the story of the postmodern, post-industrialized, post-Christian 'sinless' self and the story of atonement played out in the Passion Narrative. Alan Mann charts a way through the apparent impasse between a story that supposedly relies on sin and guilt to become meaningful, and one that fails to recognize the plight of humanity as portrayed in this way. He shows how the biblical narrative needs to be reread in the light of this emerging story so that it can speak meaningfully and sufficiently to an increasingly 'sinless' society.

'Clear, creative, deep, compelling and inspiring' – **Brian D. McLaren**, author, speaker, networker

'Alan Mann's voice is needed and welcome . . . A penetrating analysis of the world we inhabit.' – **Joel B. Green**, Asbury Theological Seminary

'An insightful, timely and creative view of the atonement for our postmodern times.' – **Steve Chalk**, Oasis Trust

978-1-84227-355-5

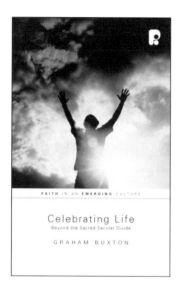

Celebrating Life

Beyond the Sacred-Secular Divide

Graham Buxton

As Christians, our engagement with the world and with culture is often impoverished as a result of unbiblical dualisms. More than we realise, the divide between sacred and secular is reinforced in our minds, contributing to an unhealthy and, at times, narrow super-spirituality. Seeking a more postmodern, holistic and, ultimately, more *Christian* approach to culture, Graham Buxton leads us on a journey towards the celebration of life in *all* its dimensions.

The first part of the book examines the roots of our dualistic thinking and its implications for culture. Part Two draws us from dualism to holism in a number of chapters that consider our engagement with literature, the creative arts, science, politics and business. Part Three draws the threads together by setting out the dimensions of a more holistic theology of the church's engagement with, and participation in, contemporary society that will lead us 'beyond the sacred-secular divide'.

> 'This is incarnational theology at its best!' – **Ray S. Anderson**, Senior Professor of Theology and Ministry, Fuller Theological Seminary, California.

Graham Buxton is Director of Postgraduate Studies in Ministry and Theology, Tabor College, Adelaide, Australia. He is author of Dancing in the Dark and The Trinity, Creation and Pastoral Ministry.

978-1-84227-507-1

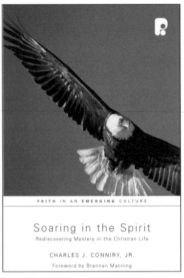

Soaring in the Spirit

Rediscovering Mystery in the Christian Life

Charles J. Conniry, Jr.

This is a book about experiencing the presence of Jesus Christ in the moment-by-moment 'nows' of daily life. James McClendon, Jr. observed that the first task of theology is to locate our place in the story. Like finding directions at a shopping mall with the brightly coloured words, 'you are here,' the author invites us into an encounter with the 'we-are-here' place in God's Great Story. The claim of this book is that the experience of Christ's presence in the 'right-here' of our daily walk – *Christian soaring* – is the birthright of every follower of Jesus Christ. This is a thoughtful, stirring, and ground-breaking book on the neglected topic of *Christian soaring through discerning discipleship*.

> 'This book is a *tour de force* . . . and can be read with profit by believers and unbelievers, philosophers and theologians, pastors and lay people, and anyone who longs to soar in the Spirit . . . It not only blessed me but drew me to prayer.' – **Brennan Manning**, author of *The Ragamuffin Gospel*.

Charles J. Conniry, Jr. is Associate Professor of Pastoral Ministry and Director of the Doctor of Ministry Program at George Fox Evangelical Seminary, Portland.

978-1-84227-508-5

Forthcoming Series Titles

Chrysalis

The Hidden Transformation in the Journey of Faith

Alan Jamieson

Increasing numbers of Christian people find their faith metamorphosing. Substantial and essential change seems to beckon them beyond the standard images and forms of Christian faith but questions about where this may lead remain. Is this the death of personal faith or the emergence of something new? Could it be a journey that is Spirit-led?

Chrysalis uses the life-cycle of butterflies as a metaphor for the faith journey that many contemporary people are experiencing. Drawing on the three main phases of a butterfly's life and the transformations between these, the book suggests subtle similarities with the zones of Christian faith that many encounter. For butterflies and Christians change between these *'phases'* or *'zones'* is substantial, life-changing and irreversible.

This book accompanies ordinary people in the midst of substantive faith change. It is an excellent resource for those who choose to support others through faith transformations. *Chrysalis* is primarily pastoral and practical drawing on the author's experience of accompanying people in the midst of difficult personal faith changes.

Alan Jamieson is a minister in New Zealand and a trained sociologist. His internationally acclaimed first book, *A Churchless Faith*, researched why people leave their churches to continue their walk of faith outside the church.

978-1-84227-544-3

FAITH IN AN EMERGING CULTURE

Metavista:
Bible, Church and Mission in an Age of Imagination

COLIN GREENE & MARTIN ROBINSON

the church after postmodernity

Metavista

Bible, Church and Mission in an Age of Imagination

Colin Green and Martin Robinson

The core narrative of the Christian faith, the book that conveys it (the Bible) and the institution of the church have all been marginalised by the development of modernity and post-modernity. Strangely, post-modernity has created an opportunity for religious thinking and experience to re-enter the lives of many. Yet, despite its astonishing assault on modernity, post-modernity is not itself an adequate framework for thinking about life. There is therefore a new opportunity for Christians to imagine what comes *after* post-modernity and to prepare the church, its book and its story for a new engagement of mission with western culture. The church on the margins, through a creative missionary imagination can audaciously re-define the centre of western cultural life. This book will attempt to sketch what such an approach might look like

'If you have a taste for the subversive, a passion for the church, a heart for biblical engagement, and an eye on the future; this book is a must-read.'
– **Roy Searle**, Northumbria Community, former President of the Baptist Union of Great Britain

Colin Greene is Professor of Theological and Cultural Studies at Mars Hill Graduate School in Seattle. He is author of *Christology in Cultural Perspective.*
Martin Robinson is an international speaker, a writer, and Director of 'Together in Mission'.

978-1-84227-506-1